Praise for *We Thin*

M000103961

"Why didn't I have a copy of *We Think With Ink* when I was teaching? Michael Leannah's book is more than a compendium of innovative ideas to motivate children's writing, it is a treasure house of why and how we teach children to be fluent writers. His varied lessons support both students and teachers with modeling and effective strategies for success."
— Linda Pils, teacher, writer, reading/language arts consultant, co-director of the Wisconsin Writing Project

"This book is a glimpse into the world of master teacher Michael Leannah as he shares the amazing benefits of writing, both in and out of the classroom. Leannah has been instrumental in ensuring the success of thousands of students over his career."
— Dr. Ted DiStefano, middle school principal

"*We Think With Ink* is a clearly-written companion to any writing curriculum. The author provides engaging lessons, examples, word games, and tips designed to help us motivate and increase self-confidence in our student writers. He encourages educators to reflect on our own attitudes and approaches to writing, and reminds us of the power we have to show kids how fun writing can be."
— Lou Ann Van Wyk, classroom teacher

"This book reads like a celebration of the act of writing, which is refreshing. Leannah's love of writing and teaching have led him to create lessons that young writers — and their teachers — will enjoy. *We Think With Ink* is the type of reference book educators return to again and again."
— Jamie A. Swenson, author, librarian, writing coach, MFA in writing

"So many books on writing outline the basic facts about what to teach and when. The great thing about *We Think With Ink* is that it tells why we should write. For every exercise or lesson provided in the book, a credible and often entertaining reason to learn the skill is also provided. This book is going to be my go-to resource for a long time to come."
— Jeremy Kimble, AMI Montessori director, certified special education teacher

"Michael Leannah's vast experience as a teacher is evident in his nuts-and-bolts writing activities and procedures in *We Think With Ink*. Teachers will find it easy to implement his ideas in their classrooms. My copy is full of yellow sticky notes marking ideas to incorporate into my writing lessons!"
— Kris Gerke Komes, teacher of English as a Second Language

"Reading this book is like having a conversation with the author, and it's a real pleasure 'talking' with someone so immensely knowledgeable."
— Julie Hauck, classroom teacher

"I wish Michael Leannah's *We Think With Ink* could be in every classroom. The entire book is jam-packed with clear, concise (and fun!) strategies for instilling in students a love of words. Warning: Leannah's enthusiasm for writing is highly contagious!"
— Jill Esbaum, children's book author

"With numerous activities and lots of helpful advice given in a voice that is always warm, encouraging, and wise, Michael Leannah's *We Think With Ink* is the kind of book I wish I'd had when I began teaching creative writing almost twenty years ago. Everything from classroom materials, writing exercises, illustrations of the writing process, and even suggestions for submitting work are covered here. This book is a benefit to writing students of all ages."
— Stephen Powers, associate professor of English at Gordon State College, author of *The Follower's Tale*

"*We Think With Ink* is filled with innovative and fun ideas to teach writing skills for every level of students. Everything from vocabulary, to composition, to publishing is covered in this book in unique and engaging ways."
— Cheryl Blahnik, classroom teacher, reading specialist, and ESL teacher

"*We Think With Ink* is a wonderful resource for both beginning and experienced teachers. It provides quick and easy strategies to establish a positive writing environment for students. I'm excited to try Leannah's games, activities, and "idea seeds" in my classroom!"
— Lisa Pelland, classroom teacher

"Michael Leannah's voice rings out loud and clear as an advocate for student writers and their teachers in this enthusiastic handbook for building a classroom writing program. *We Think With Ink* has practical advice and actionable ideas, but it also stresses the importance of helping students develop a positive connection to the creative power of the writing process."
— Duane Steen, Early Literacy Intervention teacher

"*We Think With Ink* reveals a joy for language and word play that teachers and children alike are craving. I didn't even know I was looking for this book, but it has renewed my spark to make writing fun for my students. I can incorporate so many of the ideas into my daily lessons as we find special authors in all of us!"
— Susan Schwiebert, classroom teacher

"A treasure trove of ideas for both new and experienced writing teachers. It made me smile to find some of the exact games and activities I did over the years with my students. And it also made me smile to see so many creative and instructive activities I never did, which I wish I had known about!"
— Helaine Kriegel, emerita faculty, University of Wisconsin-Madison ESL Program

"*We Think With Ink* is a must-have for any teacher hoping to grow writers in the classroom. It is brimming with examples and practical ideas for fostering daily writing. The intimidation of filling a blank page will disappear as students are guided toward becoming authors."
— Jeanne Pfeiffer, instructor and supervisor, University of Wisconsin-Oshkosh

WE THINK WITH INK

TEACHING (AND REACHING) YOUNG PEOPLE
THROUGH WRITING-CENTERED INSTRUCTION

Michael Leannah

Illustrations by
Willa Leannah

ISBN-13: 978-0997976502
ISBN-10: 0997976500

Contents

For all my students over the years.
Thank you for all you have taught me.

How to Use This Book

We Think With Ink® was developed for teachers who see creative writing as a way to maximize:

1) all literary skills
2) student self-esteem and self-worth
3) retention of daily lessons across the curriculum
4) organizational skills
5) social skills and interpersonal communication

A teacher embracing this program will emphasize creative writing throughout the school day, incorporating writing into all subject areas.

The activities and projects in this program are designed to be open-ended and flexible, making them especially conducive to reaching *all* students, including those with special needs, the gifted and talented, and the emotionally challenged.

We Think With Ink® is to be used as a supplement to the existing classroom reading and writing programs. It is also recommended for use as a textbook/workbook in a school writing center, the centerpiece of a home school approach to writing instruction, or as a guidebook for individuals honing writing skills independently.

Paper and Pen vs. Computer Keyboard

While students with limited fine motor skills may prefer the keyboard, *We Think With Ink* works best with pen or pencil on paper. Something special happens with the physical act of writing: a connection between the brain and the heart of the writer through the grinding of the graphite against the surface of the paper. As messy as some of our handwriting might be, it is ours, as distinct as our signature, a vital part of each of us.

> *"How can I know what I think*
> *till I see what I say?"*
> — E. M. Forster

CHAPTER 1

Why We Write

We think with ink. Ink in pens, printers, and markers. "Ink" in pencils and in paint. In chalk on a sidewalk. In a stick scrawling words in the sand. In a finger writing a message in the dust on a shelf.

We do our best thinking when our thoughts are written down. A great power is unleashed through the act of writing: the grasping of a pencil, the friction of the pen point on a paper's surface, the feel of keys under our fingertips, the tactile experience of slathering paint on a canvas. Something magical happens when a thought is written down. The thought becomes *real*.

Thoughts flit about in our minds, flickering and flashing like streaks of lightning in an electrical storm. Here's a thought. Now it's gone. Here's another. Poof. Disappeared.

But write down a thought and you've got it. It's captured, and it won't get away. An idea for an invention. A joke you don't want to forget. The plot of a story you plan to write, a rhythmic combination of words for a poem, an idea for a character in a play. Once written, a thought is a concrete object that can be stored and used and shared.

Often, the difference between thinking and writing is the difference between nothing and something.

Every one of us is constantly thinking, making resolutions, setting goals. But thoughts are fleeting, like clouds in the wind, soon scattered and gone. We jump from idea to memory to goal to worry to another goal another memory another thought. Hop, leap, jump.

If we don't write down what we are thinking, our thoughts and dreams and resolutions won't amount to much.

An artist envisions a seaside with crashing waves in the moonlight, but if paint isn't put to the canvas, the beach and the waves and the moonlight do not exist in tangible form. An image in the brain of a sculptor has permanence only after she carves it into a statue. And a story rattling around in the mind of a writer is nothing until it is given form with letters, words, and sentences.

We write notes to ourselves so we don't forget important dates and events. We jot messages to family members, reminding them of our plans and thoughts ("I won't be home until after five." "Don't forget your doctor's appointment in the morning." "I love you."). These examples of writing won't win literary awards, but they are important to us in our daily lives.

We remember better if we write down our thoughts, goals, and aspirations. Something as simple as a grocery list helps us to remember what it is we need from the store. If I don't take the time to write a list…

…I'll find myself standing in the grocery store wondering what it was I came to get. Funny thing is, when I do write down the items, I don't need to look at the list in my pocket. *Because I wrote them down*, I remember them. The physical writing of the words makes an indelible imprint on the brain.

It is true: We think with ink.

The "Contagious" Teacher

In *We Think With Ink*, the teacher's most important task is to engender in her students a love for words and writing. A positive attitude toward reading and writing is contagious. From day one, demonstrate and encourage playfulness with words and sentences. That means occasionally using outrageous puns and repeating such old refrains as "How much wood would a woodchuck chuck if a woodchuck could chuck wood?"

There are three types of teachers in a *We Think With Ink* classroom: 1) Someone who has been published. (Even having a small article published in a local magazine or newspaper will excite and motivate kids.) 2) Someone who personally knows a published writer. (If a friend from your college days is now an author, refer to him often, and use him as a model for your students.) 3) Someone who has good knowledge of a well-known author or two. (Most teachers fall in this third category.) It is good for your students to know of your admiration for an author. Know the story of that author and refer to it often.

The teacher's enthusiasm for writing is essential.

Motivating Your Students

Molding a Lump of Clay

Imagine: You are a teacher standing in front of a class of twenty-five students. You give to each student a small lump of clay. Each lump is equal in size and weight.

"Make something with your lump of clay," you tell the students. "Mold it. Shape it. Make something. If you don't like what you first see, mash it back into a ball and start over. I want to see something interesting in fifteen minutes."

When time is up, you examine the finished products. One boy has made a bowl-shaped object. "What is it?" you ask. "It's a bowl," he says.

The next student has also made a bowl, but this one is bigger, its walls thinner. Someone on the other side of the room says, "I have a bowl, too," and you compare the three bowls, each unique.

But not everyone has made a bowl. One boy is busy putting the finishing touches on an intricate space ship with missile launchers lining the tapered wings. A girl has made a bust of Beethoven. Another girl has divided her clay into eight separate parts and has shaped the parts into pieces of fruit.

Now imagine this: You are a teacher and you are giving your students a writing assignment. "Write about a memory you have of a time when you felt enormously proud." (Note: Because the students begin with different vocabularies and background knowledge, the "lumps" this time are not equal.)

After the allotted time, you collect the papers. The first one is from a girl who tells of hitting a home run in the bottom of the ninth to win the championship for her team. A boy's paper is next, and he tells of a time when he

11

saved his grandmother's life by running to a neighbor's house to get help. The next boy describes his reaction to loud applause after playing a guitar solo at the school talent show. That one is followed by a girl telling of the time she chased off a bully who was hurting someone smaller.

The similarities between the clay project and the writing assignment are clear. In both, students are given a "lump" to work with, a kernel of an idea that in the beginning has no shape or form. But a finished product is molded, shaped, and worked until its meaning can be recognized by a viewer/reader.

> *"There are a thousand thoughts lying within a man*
> *that he does not know till he takes up a pen to write."*
> — *William Makepeace Thackeray*

Here's the problem: Most kids would consider the clay activity fun, something they could do as well as anyone else in the room. "You made a bust of Beethoven? Nice. Look at the unicorn I made."

The writing assignment? The feeling is *not necessarily* the same. Some of the students *might* approach the writing activity with less self-confidence. They *might* feel that no matter what they write, it will compare poorly with others in the class. Writing a story, for some kids, is hard, not fun. Unchecked, this negative feeling feeds the great misconception that kids hate writing, which is one of the biggest obstacles we writing teachers face and must overcome.

Our task is to help the students to embrace writing as a desirable activity, something they look forward to doing every day. Good news: This mission will have already been accomplished if your current students had a teacher in the past who showed them that writing is fun.

If that has indeed been done for them, you won't be hearing the "I hate writing" mantra, because the fact is, **kids don't hate writing**, but they do need someone to show them that they don't. If no prior teacher took care of this for your students, the honor falls to you this year.

A related stumbling block exists in the fact that many teachers see the teaching of writing as a difficult part of the daily curriculum. Anything presented poorly will appear to be unpleasant. Changes in attitude and approach will allow you to take a giant step over all the obstacles.

12

We Think With Ink

Some teachers say they have no time for writing instruction, that their plates are always too full. Writing assignments, if done properly, can free up minutes in the classroom.

> *The idea that kids naturally loathe writing is hogwash, as ridiculous as saying they don't enjoy talking or thinking.*

Perhaps someday every school will have a writing lab, staffed by a full-time, well-qualified writing specialist. We can wish. Most schools, of course, do not have such a room, so we teachers are left to fit writing assignments into the cracks of our schedules as best we can. *We Think With Ink* is all about recognizing those cracks and gaps, and fitting our assignments into them.

Many of the activities and word games in this book can be played in five minutes here, ten minutes there, while you're waiting for stragglers to come in in the morning, or for the lunch bell to ring — time that is frequently squandered.

You don't need a lot of time to ask a quick question that leads to several kids getting a boost in self-esteem. When a breakdown occurs in class — someone is angry and lashing out, or expressing sadness over an unfortunate event at home — a short writing assignment can lead to meaningful discussion, problem solving, the sorting out of hurt feelings.

As a way of reinforcing the day's lesson in science, social studies, or math, a writing assignment is given, worked on, and shared. The writing assignment is *part of* the science lesson, *part of* the social studies class, not a separate load of work searching for a sliver of schedule to squeeze itself into uncomfortably.

Teachers often shudder at the thought of assigning written work because they envision themselves spending entire evenings reading endless stacks of papers and writing out lengthy comments. *We Think With Ink* is based on students learning how to check and analyze their own and each other's papers much of the time. For a good number of the assignments, the students will have the option of not turning the papers in to the teacher at all.

Please tell yourself that the days of approaching writing instruction as if it were a sink full of dirty dishes, something icky that needs to be done, are *gone*. Your students will not have to be coaxed and prodded into writing a good story. With the right approach, motivating young writers is like operating an automatic dishwasher. Push the right buttons and the task is accomplished with ease. And joy.

Five Keys to Getting Off on the Right Foot

1. Assume that each of your students has creativity and talent. Do not make the mistake of thinking they cannot write or don't want to write. A baseball coach doesn't expect his new players to be no good. On the first day of practice he wants to see their strengths, and he assumes they have some. You should feel that way about each of your students.

2. Hit the ground running. Give the class a fun, rousing assignment right at the start. Get them going.

3. Establish the practice of critiquing. A critique is a detailed review of a piece of writing. Yes, writing is primarily a solitary endeavor, but other eyes must see a writer's work. In learning to critique each other's papers, your students will come to excel at examining and editing their own stories.

4. Set publication as the goal for the class. People outside the classroom will read your students' stories.

5. Emphasize the importance of recognizing the *strengths* in the stories produced in class. Your students will nod their heads at good, strong characters, interesting plot ideas, and deliciously descriptive words. They will learn to be like the man who looks out the window and sees the sunshine on the flowers, the playful puppy in the grass, the birds zinging from branch to branch in the trees…and doesn't even notice the litter blowing in the street.

The main thrust of *We Think With Ink* is the writing of stories and poems. While nonfiction is not to be ignored, **our primary emphasis is on fiction**. Remember: *We Think With Ink* supplements the existing reading and language programs, reinforcing and providing opportunities to apply the subject matter learned in class.

Where writing is concerned, we want students to see the big picture. Writing is a means of expression, a vehicle for self-evaluation, a method of encapsulating the whole of instruction and displaying it in a meaningful manner and form.

Grading of stories can be implemented, but is not vital. When real authors finish writing a book, they don't seek out approval or a grade from an outside source. They relish the feeling that wells up from within after the work is done. They acknowledge the reactions and compliments of their readers. And they get busy on their next story. (See more about grading in Chapter 9.)

> *When you write a story or a poem, a special kind of magic happens. Whole worlds that didn't exist an hour ago are now taking shape. You — the writer — create the characters and the worlds in which they live. You think up the situations and make your characters struggle. You decide, good or bad, what happens to your characters in the end.*

Your students will be excited about what they are creating on the page. Before long they will be clamoring for attention after writing a funny story, a lively poem, something that makes them feel involved and proud. They will be like kids calling to their moms and dads at a swimming pool: "Look at me!" they shout as they jump from the diving board, swim from one side of the pool to the other, plunge face-first into the water. In your writing class, the writers will want everyone to "Look at me!" when it's time to have the stories read aloud.

You hold the key to your students being motivated to write such stories. An ideal writing prompt (at *We Think With Ink* we call prompts "idea seeds") can turn a class of reluctant writers into a roomful of would-be Louisa May Alcotts and Stephen Kings. (See more about "idea seeds" in Chapter 3.)

Publishing Students' Writing

Most of us will never make speeches to crowds of thousands, but we still want to speak well when we express ourselves verbally. In the same way, we may not be award-winning authors, but we want our writing to be done well. Even a kid's note left on the kitchen table for Mom ought to be written correctly.

We don't learn a skill and then keep our talents hidden. Those who learn to play the clarinet or the piano are expected to demonstrate their skills at recitals. Basketball players practice, then perform in games in front of the crowd. In the *We Think With Ink* classroom, students strive to see their written work published — put in a form so others will read it. **Our goal is to have others read our work.** An important part of *We Think With Ink* is to have the writing published in some form, and read.

We make booklets that find a place on a shelf in the school library. We produce monthly compilations of stories and poems that are distributed in the community or sent home for families to read and enjoy. Collections of stories are printed and given to friends and family as gifts. We send our written work to real newspapers, Facebook pages, and blogs.

Consider sending some of the class's very best writing to magazine and book publishers that accept submissions from young people. Be on the lookout for companies, websites, and TV shows that sponsor contests for young writers. It is great fun for the whole class when someone in the group is entered in a contest. (It's also exciting for the kids when their teacher actively markets his work and keeps them informed of the progress.)

> *"If there's a book that you want to read, but it hasn't been written yet, then you must write it."*
> — *Toni Morrison*

To publish a real book — the kind found in a library or book store — usually means something must happen in a faraway, Emerald City-like place. Your students should know there is a yellow-brick road that can lead to that place. "It's a long road, with lots of pitfalls and times of discouragement, and when you finally get there, they might not open the door to you. But it's still a lot of fun to try." (See Chapter 8 for more on getting published.)

From Writing Skills to Reading Skills

You can learn how baseball is played by reading a rule book. To better understand, you could watch a game being played. But to *really* understand the game, you ought to *play the game*. **The closer you get to the real action, the better you'll understand.** The same is true with literary skills — writing and reading.

A child listens as a story is read aloud, and her imagination is sparked. In her head, rain is pelting the windows of a dark and spooky house, horses gallop, candles flicker, waves crash onto the rocks on the shoreline. Without even knowing it, the listener develops a lifelong love for language. She acquires a sense for the way words and sentences are pieced together and how a good story is constructed. She feels a closeness to the author of the story, to the person reading, to others in the room who are listening.

Imagine that child now a little older, reading the book to herself. Her imagination allowed to run free, she pauses frequently in her reading to let mental images play out. She rereads sections that resonate. In seeing the words, she comes to appreciate the workings of language ten times more than when she was merely listening. The bond with a reader no longer exists, but the closeness she had with the author is even greater now. And she now has a bond with herself, a feeling of great satisfaction in being able to do the reading.

Now picture the child one more time, older still, at a desk writing a story of her own. She creates her own characters, devises her own plots, fixes her own conclusions. *Magic is happening.* Her understanding of the language takes her to places she never knew existed. There is neither a bond with an outside reader nor an outside author anymore, but the *bond with herself* is something truly beautiful. She sees herself as someone knowledgeable, competent, and creative.

Can someone know how to write well and not also know how to *read* well? The answer is no. **If we want young readers to really know how to read, we need to help them to really know how to write.**

Chapter 2

The Most Effective Classroom Environment

Whether it's a formal writing lab in a school, a classroom designed for an emphasis on writing, or a child's bedroom at home, the room where an aspiring writer works ought to be set up with care. Nothing expensive or complicated is needed. The goal, simply put, is to immerse the young writer in letters, words, sentences, and stories. To create a good writer's environment, your main needs are imagination and resourcefulness. And don't lose sight of the fact that the teacher's overall attitude is always more important than the materials in the room.

Make the room an inviting place, with the walls covered with the names and pictures of authors, writing rules, and samples of excellent writing. Always keep your eyes open at thrift stores and rummage sales, excellent places to find not only pencils, pens, paper, and books, but games and game-making materials, as well as small prizes to be awarded to the winners of games played in class. Accept cast-off supplies from teachers cleaning out their classroom cupboards. Be ready when the school library discards unwanted books and magazines. You cannot accomplish everything all at once, but by your second or third year, you will have a wonderful assortment of writing-themed resources and supplies.

As an art room is filled with art-related materials and equipment, fill your classroom with the tools and provisions used by writers. Paper and writing utensils, of course. Scissors, staplers, and other book-making tools are also necessary. Shelves full of books and magazines for reading and reference are essential. Yes, computers, scanners, and printers have a place, but so do old-fashioned dictionaries and thesauruses. The tactile aspects of writing are important. Again, think of the typical art room that, even in our digital world, still makes good use of paints and clay.

Maximize the available space in the room for storage. Again, thrift stores and rummage sales are good places to find cheap shelving, bins, cupboards, and drawers. You will need to have space for writing supplies: paper, pens, scissors, paper clips.

In an art room, every little piece of pipe cleaner and scrap of foil is kept for collage projects and other purposes. In your writing-centered classroom, be just as careful about throwing away useful "junk." Old encyclopedia sets and tattered magazines are extremely valuable. The covers of student-created books can be made beautiful with pieces of colored sticky paper, yarn, and glittery doo-dads. Think twice before throwing away such items.

Keep a supply of old picture frames of different sizes. A poem in a frame looks good on display in the classroom or as a gift to someone special.

An assortment of books in the classroom is essential. Books about writing are always good, but mainly you want books that your aspiring authors can read and take apart, praise, question, and criticize. We writers learn from other writers, taking what we like and rejecting what we don't like. Without realizing it, young writers learn how to write by reading.

Good Daily Practices

Use your chalkboard or white board often. Many of us are visual learners and we want to see sentences and paragraphs, not just hear them read. Remember, too, that some of the best writing assignments begin with class discussions. These can take place with students sitting at their desks or facing each another in a discussion circle. Be prepared to move desks or classroom furniture to accommodate this activity, or designate an area of the room for this purpose.

Daily Question

Start the day with a question on the board for your students to consider when they enter. Each student writes an answer to the question in his notebook. After attendance is taken, the class shares and discusses. The whole activity takes just five or ten minutes, but it gets the class thinking, writing, listening, and sharing.

Here are some examples of Daily Questions that I have used. (More can be found in Appendix 2.) Remember that the answers to these questions could change from day to day, so reuse the questions occasionally.

What are you looking forward to doing later today?

What is making you nervous about next week?
What happened the last time you felt proud of someone in your family?
What is your favorite memory from yesterday?
Who is the person you most admire?

Writing Portfolios

Each student should keep a writing portfolio. Not all writing assignments need to be kept. Students will want to save their best or most significant assignments. I suggest requiring each student to have at least 12 writing assignments placed in the portfolio per quarter. If the portfolio has two pockets, one can be used for "unfinished stories." Writing assignments should always be dated for later reference. When put in order, progress will be evident. The portfolios will be useful at conference time.

Fix-It Sentences

Sometimes, for a break in the action, draw attention to the board where you have written three Fix-It Sentences. The students are to read the sentences and determine what, if anything, is wrong with them, then rewrite the sentences in their notebooks, fixed properly. A wise philosopher once said, "If it ain't broke, don't fix it," so sentences written correctly are to be left alone. Different writers will edit incorrect sentences in different ways, so it is important to compare and discuss when doing Fix-It Sentences.

This activity allows for the students to "play the teacher," analyzing sentences and making appropriate corrections. Some students will enjoy coming up with Fix-It Sentences of their own to challenge the class. (See more Fix-It Sentences in Appendix 4.)

Communication with the Teacher

Give your students a chance to communicate with you through writing. I found an old-fashioned rural mail box at a rummage sale and used it in my classroom for this purpose. When someone placed a note or letter inside the box, they raised the little flag on the side and I knew that someone had something to tell me. I responded promptly with a note passed during lunch or some such time. (If a real mailbox is not available, a decorated shoe box will suffice.)

About once a month, I passed out slips to my students and asked them to tell me three things about themselves that they wanted me to know, or that they thought I ought to know. I explained that this was a chance to brag a little, to complain, or to reveal something difficult. In the rush of the day, students sometimes don't have the opportunity to share news concerning personal troubles, worries, and concerns (divorce, sickness in the family, older siblings moving away, etc.). I have found this simple practice of offering the chance to "write three things" to be very important and meaningful.

Another good written communication vehicle is the "Reporting Station." Keep three jars or boxes marked "Compliments," "Complaints," and "Explanations." Respectful notes are welcome and will be read at the end of the day. If anyone has a good word to say, here's your chance to communicate it. Have a complaint? Let us know; maybe we can help. Are you feeling misunderstood? Do you need to explain why you did something that others are questioning? Write it up and put the slip in the box.

Use of a Timer

A kitchen timer, the kind used for timing cakes or cookies in the oven, is a useful tool in the writing-centered classroom. In the early weeks of the year, before the students have learned what it takes to be a good writer, use the timer to encourage them to work longer and harder on their stories.

Initially, too many young writers want to rush and be done with their assignments. Set the timer and give points toward a reward for any writers still writing when the bell rings.

For a class with students who need help with staying on task, set the timer for an unknown length — two minutes, five minutes, thirty seconds — and get the writers started on their assignments. If all the students are on task when the bell rings, the class earns a point toward a reward.

The Classroom Workshop

Perhaps a table or a few extra chairs in the back of the room can be what you will call the "Classroom Workshop," a place where students can find materials and tools to make booklets, posters, cards, and other writing projects.

In bins, drawers, or boxes, keep the following supplies handy: paper (blank, lined, graph, construction), pens, pencils, erasers, crayons, envelopes, note cards, sticky notes, clips and fasteners, staplers, rulers, scissors, paint, and glue.

Don't forget newspapers and magazines to be cut and pasted for projects. Dictionaries and thesauruses too.

Keep a collection of writing samples from newspaper or magazine advertisements, letters to the editor, movie reviews, travel brochures, song lyrics, and invitations. Point out that someone *was paid* for writing those instructions, that menu, the back of that cereal box.

Booklet Making

A simple booklet can be made with as few as three short stories, printed or written neatly, bound with staples or fasteners inside a colorful cover. These booklets can be shared, traded, or given as gifts to family or friends. Sometimes a group of students can make a book together, with each contributing a story or two on a particular theme ("Christmas Stories," "Animal Poems").

These booklets are the surest way for a student's writing to be published. And, yes, we do consider this publishing because these books will be read by people outside the walls of the classroom.

Each month, three or four students can be assigned the task of compiling and making a class booklet of stories and poems which will be placed in the school library and distributed to other teachers in the school. A copy will also go home with each student in the class, so families will be able to read the class's best work each month.

Stories written by the teacher can be included in the booklets as well. Imagine the effect your stories will have on your students. If you grew up on a farm, for instance, your students will be delighted to read about your memories of caring for the cows and the chickens. And won't they love reading about the time you dealt so well with that bully at school when you were their age.

A Vocabulary Booklet

Everyone in class, even the teacher, should make a booklet for unknown words. Label the pages A through Z. As you're reading and come to words whose meanings you do not know (or don't know how to pronounce), jot them into the Vocabulary Booklet. Later, look up the words and write clues for yourself so you'll remember them the next time you meet them. Brush up on the words in the booklet frequently, until you know them well.

"A Book of Positives," "A Funny Book," etc.

Make a booklet. Put the title on the cover. Write the first page. Give the book to someone in the class. Tell that person to write the second page and to then pass it to someone else to write the next page, and to keep this up until the booklet is finished.

For example, here is Page 1 of "A Book of Positives": "I saw Joshua G. this morning helping his little sister when she fell off her bike. She was scared more than hurt, and that's why Joshua helped her more than a doctor could have. He lifted her up and brushed her off and checked her knees for cuts. I couldn't hear what he was saying to her, but whatever it was, I could tell that she liked it. I have a big brother, and when I was little he helped me too. He still helps me today sometimes. And I help him whenever I can. I loved seeing Joshua helping his sister this morning."

Sometimes an unfinished booklet is given to someone who has nothing to add. He will keep the booklet until he has something to write. Sometimes it takes weeks to complete a booklet.

Anyone can start a booklet like this. "A Funny Book" gets started when someone writes a joke or a story about something funny that happened. "A Book of Wisdom" will include stories about people being wise and thoughtful. It might include sayings from famous thinkers, or messages from students who have something wise to share with others.

Card Making

"Get Well" cards, "Birthday" cards, and cards of friendship or congratulations can be made in the classroom workshop. This is a good alternative for a student who finds himself in trouble at school. "Your muddy boots made a mess in the hallway this morning? Make a card of apology for the custodian." "You said something to hurt your friend's feelings? Tell him how you feel in a card."

Activity Sheets and Playing Cards

At the classroom workshop, activity sheets for games and other activities can be created and made available for all to use. Worksheets with 26 boxes (one for each letter of the alphabet) are always in demand. Sheets with 5x5 grids (or grids of other dimensions) are frequently needed too. Also recommended are sheets with two columns of blanks, for lists of synonyms, antonyms, homophones, and other word pairs.

Decks of cards can be used for countless games and activities. Several games involve number cards, while other games require letter cards or word cards. Homemade cards for such games get worn out quickly. New decks will need to be produced regularly.

Word Walls

Use the wall (and even the ceiling) space in your classroom. I like to see many different word walls in a classroom, each one growing and changing day by day. Word lists can be strung by thread and dangled from the ceiling. (Be careful. String danglers can trigger some security systems' motion detectors.) The lists are there for reference as students write, aiding them in finding good words and in spelling correctly without consulting the dictionary.

Be careful of word walls becoming overcrowded or full of "dead" information so familiar that no one pays attention to it anymore. To fix this problem, at the end of each quarter, assign a student or two to condense the best of what is there to a page or two. Keep the pages inside a folder for later reference. Then clear the space for new information.

Ideas for Word Walls and Bulletin Boards

Challenge Words

Challenge Words are long words that we don't use every day but are fun to know. Everyone in class should be on the lookout for words to add to the list. Here are a few to get you started:

Ambidextrous: the ability to use the left and right hands equally well.
Ambrosia: food that smells and tastes very good.
Babushka: a triangular fabric head covering.
Boondoggle: an impractical or wasteful piece of business or activity.
Clishmaclaver: gossip; foolish talk.
Dodecahedron: a solid figure having twelve sides.
Gorgonzola: an Italian cheese.
Hobbledehoy: an awkward young fellow.
Logomania: a strong interest in words.
Persnickety: extremely fussy about small details.
Tintinnabulation: the ringing, jingling, or tinkling of bells.

Your students' families will be very impressed when they hear the Challenge Words being used in casual conversation at the dinner table. "What is this ambrosia we're having tonight?" (Can toasted cheese sandwiches and baked beans be considered ambrosia? Yes, of course.) "I can't wait until Saturday so I won't have to hear the tintinnabulation of my alarm clock in the morning." But be sure to warn your students that using Challenge Words can sometimes cause problems. A kid who says, "My teacher thinks I have logomania," might be rushed to the hospital.

Trouble Words

These words cause us trouble because they are so difficult to know how to use. People have been struggling with them for ages. Any one of the examples from this list could be chosen for analysis when you have a need to fill two or three minutes at the end of class, or any other time you desire. As with the other word walls, additions can be made to this list daily.

altogether/all together	dessert/desert	lose/loose
accept/except	affect/effect	bin/been
medal/metal/meddle/mettle	besides/beside	bring/take
among/between	fewer/less	good/well
leave/let	than/then	them/those
can hardly/can't hardly	learn/teach	in to/into
there/their/they're	lend/borrow	lie/lay

Puns

Puns are jokes with words that sound alike or mean more than one thing. "What is purple and 5000 miles long? The Grape Wall of China." "I can't go fast on my bike because it is two-tired." Make a word wall with words that could be made into puns.

(See more Bulletin Board/Word Wall ideas in Appendix 5.)

Chapter 3

Reaching All Students: the Gifted, the Troubled, and Those in Between

Setting the Stage

We Think With Ink works particularly well in a classroom with students of varying needs. Minimal differentiation of assignments is required. All students work with the same prompt, or idea seed; at most, the directions may have to be presented in a variety of ways for students with different needs.

Once the members of your class come to know each other and accept one another as a critique group "family," you're already halfway home. With each assignment, all students start with the same idea seed and develop something unique. When it is time to share, not just the complex and colorful stories produced by the high achievers are admired. Stories penned by less advanced writers are recognized for creativity and insight as well.

The *We Think With Ink* way of writing fiction opens doors to the introspective, the emotionally challenged, and those with poor self-esteem. As a means of expression, some students find writing far more palatable and agreeable than verbalization. When speaking, there might be trouble thinking quickly and coming up with just the right words; when writing, there is time to gather one's thoughts, to sort them out, and to convey them accurately.

When a creative writer takes the point of view of someone he is not, a real freedom is unleashed. I have no illusions about *We Think With Ink* working miracles, but when I hear of a student suicide, I do wonder what might have happened if the articulation of the feelings of frustration, anger, and depression had been encouraged.

Unlike most programs designed for students with special needs, *We Think With Ink* is aimed at all students in the class. It can be used by counselors and specialists to reach the troubled and academically challenged, but it serves as well the majority in the middle. It can be a part of every class, every situation.

There are four basic goals for you as a writing teacher:

1. Generate enthusiasm for writing and for word play. The best way to do this is by your example.

2. Become a skilled editor. Develop an eye for elements of strong writing. Downplay, without ignoring, the mistakes you see. Emphasize with big red-ink stars and smiley faces all the examples of great word choice, phrasing, and sentence work. What you foster you will see more of in the writing assignments to come.

3. Be willing to accept — and promote — imperfection. The same imperfect people who have no problem singing and dancing with friends often feel that any writing they do must be perfect before they will share it. Is there such a thing as a perfect story or poem? Even the best authors have doubts about their finished works. Nothing would ever get written if we felt that only perfect stories were worth reading.

4. See that the students in your classroom a) are enjoying what they are doing, b) are feeling good about themselves, and c) are feeling comfortable and unafraid.

Early in my career as a teacher, I worked in a rough neighborhood in a large American city. Many of my second graders came to school tired, hungry, and poorly dressed. There had been trouble at home: arguments, violence, arrests. And I was supposed to tell them to open their books and get going on the math and social studies? Good luck.

I quickly learned that the day would go better if I started the morning with a self-esteem booster. Something to make us all feel better about being who and where we were. I came to be quite skilled at seamlessly incorporating those self-esteem activities into my regular lessons. Over the years, I've found myself in schools where there weren't so many "disadvantaged" kids, but kids are still kids; all have doubts and troubles and fears and insecurities. They all crave opportunities to upgrade their self-esteems.

You can't expect a young person who is fearful and apprehensive, worried, or stressed, to gladly pick up a pencil and write. Before you even try plowing ahead with your planned lesson, I advise a little ego-boosting first. Funny thing is, the ego-booster often *is* a writing assignment. Kids can unload a lot of their troubles and pain if given a piece of paper and a pen.

Writing is an outlet. And when a student's work is recognized by others for its excellence, there is no better boost to the spirit. In a writing class, the shy can show boldness, and the aggressive, sensitivity. Sometimes the kid who never speaks is the one at the end of class who can't stop writing.

If conditions are right and the perfect prompt is given, you can expect occasional magic.

Getting to Know You

For some people, sharing what they have written can be quite threatening, as scary as speaking in front of an audience. For your program to work, **you need to get to a place where your class feels good about sharing what they have written.**

Most people feel self-conscious when they first share their writing with someone new. To help your students get over such feelings, tell them to imagine twenty teenagers swimming at a lake. Is anyone watching to see who is swimming *perfectly*? Some do the backstroke well; others can do the front crawl like champions. Some swim out into the deep water while others linger near the shore. Every one of them has a style all his own. And every one of them is having fun.

The first days of class must be devoted to putting all writers at ease. Your students will be expected to share their writing with each other, so a trust must be developed among them. The goal is to reach a point where there are no worries about ridicule or embarrassment. A good first step is to provide your students with a chance to get to

29

know one another. Only after that occurs will there be any sharing of stories.

You will want to start the year with some "get to know you" activities. Have each student complete the following questionnaire called "All About You." Those who are shy or hesitant will appreciate your requiring them to write answers to just 7 of the 10 questions, if that is what they'd prefer. Notice that there aren't any "Yes or No" questions. All the questions are designed to be answered with sentences. You should not accept lazy answers, those that show little thought or effort, such as, "I like pizza because it is good," for Question #2.

All About You

1. In what cities have you lived?
2. What do you like about your favorite food?
3. What character in a book or movie do you admire?
4. What character in a book or movie scares you?
5. What character in a book or movie would you like to be for one hour?*
6. What animal would you like to be for one hour?*
7. What is your most prized possession?
8. What's the scariest or most dangerous thing you've ever done?
9. What would you say or do if you met your favorite famous person?
10. What do you think you'll be doing when you're 30 years old?

   * When asking a "What would you like to be" question, I recommend putting a time limit on it. Would I like to be a lion or a mosquito or the president of Germany, Brazil, or Zimbabwe? For an hour, maybe, but no longer than that. I'd miss my family and friends and my own life too much.

   The answers can be read aloud by the students who wrote them, or by someone else who volunteers to do the reading. Another option is to pass the papers so each student has a chance to read the others' answers.

The Lying Game

   This is a fun way for your students to get to know you, and for everyone in class to eventually get to know each other. Tell the students you are going to reveal some facts about yourself, but that you are going to mix in some lies with the facts. As you write sentences about yourself on the board, students write

30

their guesses as to which statements are true and which are lies. (Later the students can take turns being on the other end of the game, revealing true and false statements about themselves. Players must announce at the start how many sentences they are writing and how many of them will be lies. ("I have written 8 sentences and 2 of them are lies…" Any ratio is acceptable.)

The following is a list of statements about myself that I used with my seventh-grade class one year. There were eight sentences; five were true.

1. I once met someone who was in the "Wizard of Oz" movie.
2. I was on the Green Bay Packers' practice squad one summer.
3. I used to live in Milwaukee.
4. I have six children.
5. I have a dog that is fifteen years old — older than any of you.
6. I once jumped out of an airplane while it was flying.
7. I once sat across from Johnny Depp in a restaurant.
8. I am not ambidextrous.

This game can be quite fun for everyone. Even the mundane facts (I used to live in Milwaukee, etc.) provide good information that helps players get to know one another. Let's hope, however, that every player has at least one or two good juicy facts to offer. In my case, by the way, the lies were #2, #4, and #7. I did once meet a couple of the people who played Munchkins, my dog did live a long life, I did parachute from an airplane, and I am not ambidextrous — most of the kids had no idea what that word meant, but they never forgot it afterward.

Students playing this game will usually keep it simple, with a small number of facts and lies. The following example is typical, involving five sentences, three of which are true.

1. I used to live in California.
2. My grandfather won a gold medal in the Olympics a long time ago.
3. I know how to play the guitar.
4. I rode on an elephant's back in a parade.
5. I once ate a whole watermelon in one day.

6. **You get to put the hard knocks of life to good use.** Most people fail to see anything good about suffering, pain, loneliness, or sickness. Writers can use those miseries in stories. Who would want to sit in a boat with a motor that won't start, stuck on a lake in a torrential rainstorm, waiting for the Coast Guard to come to the rescue? A writer will see that horrible time as an opportunity to experience wretchedness so it can be used in a story. William Faulkner once wrote: "A writer needs three things: experience, observation, and imagination, any two of which, at times any one of which, can supply the lack of the others." Troubles often have silver linings: they help us to adjust our paths, to define ourselves, to reset our thinking and our views of the world. And they help us to write good stories.

7. **Writing creatively demands real thinking, the kind of thinking that often results in ground-shifting life changes.** All creative pursuits are good for you, but writing outshines strumming a guitar or brushing paint on a canvas. Writing makes you examine your life, your attitude, your relationships with everything around you. It can help you out of horrible predicaments, drag you out of the muck of your daily life. You can save yourself by writing.

> *"I think writing really helps you heal yourself. I think if you write long enough, you will be a healthy person."*
> — *Alice Walker*

8. **A writer with heart gives great gifts to the world.** Within your circle of family and friends, what you write and give to others is often kept. Forever. If your writing becomes published, the stories you concoct and the characters you envision are gifts you give to the world.

Getting Started

To show how a writer thinks and works, try writing a story together as a class. Once, with a group of third graders, I started by writing on the board:

We Think With Ink

"Yesterday, Christopher was walking home from school when he saw…"

I asked for someone to fill in the blank. A boy raised his hand and said, "a tiger chasing a man."

"Wow," I said as I wrote it on the board. "Does someone have a different idea? Christopher saw a…" I called on a girl this time.

"A turtle crossing the street," she said.

"I can see that in my imagination," I said as I added it to the board. "Can anyone think of a third idea?" Another girl. "A little boy crying," she said.

"Hmm," I said. "A tiger chasing a man. A turtle crossing the street. A little boy crying. Each choice would take my story in a different direction. Any one of the three will lead to an interesting story. Which one should I choose?"

Tell the class that this is how a writer thinks. She probably doesn't write the first thing that pops into her mind. She thinks of several possibilities before deciding on one. If the idea she chooses leads to a dead end, she moves to one of the other ideas, and keeps trying until one idea or another takes her story to a good place.

I chose to go with the turtle. Then I continued with:

"Oh, no! The turtle was halfway across the street when Christopher saw…"

I asked for help with what might come next.

"…a car coming."

"…a curious dog running over."

"…a big eagle swooping down."

I made a show of thinking over the possibilities before deciding on the car.

"…a car coming. It was Christopher's neighbor, Ms. Elson. 'Stop!' cried Christopher from the sidewalk. He waved his arms and jumped up and down. 'Ms. Elson, stop!'"

I looked at the class. "What happens next?"

Three ideas:

"Ms. Elson hit the brakes."

"But Ms. Elson didn't see or hear Christopher."

"Ms. Elson steered the car to the right. She missed the turtle, but her car went into the lake."

After some consideration, I took the first choice.

"The car screeched to a stop. The turtle crossed the street, tromped into the tall grass, and was gone."

The students were not only engaged in the making of a story, but were starting to see what *goes into* the making of a story. When you do this activity, let it play out as far as you want it to go, guiding it the way you would like your students to take their own stories in the days ahead.

Encourage imaginative thinking during this brain-storming activity. Tell your students that a writer's best ideas often come after all the obvious choices are considered and rejected.

With practice, you, the teacher, will get better and better at leading this activity. Mixing humor into the game is always advisable. And it's fun at the end of the activity to imagine together what would have happened to the story if you had decided to go in one of the other directions.

> *Most serious writers belong to a critique group,*
> *a group of writers (usually five or six good friends)*
> *who share their stories, ask for help, and offer*
> *suggestions for improvement. In the classroom, your*
> *students will make up a very large critique group. It*
> *will take time before everyone feels comfortable*
> *sharing, and before all become adept at writing*
> *critiques — a skill in itself. Some rules and*
> *expectations will need to be established.*
> *(For more on critiques, see Chapter 8.)*

Idea Seeds (Story Starters)

Imagine a number of dogs tied to trees, pulling, barking, fighting for release. These are your writing students, and as their teacher, your job is to unleash them. To unleash them and to run with them.

There is a simple trick to getting good stories out of young writers: Good idea seeds. I prefer "idea seed" to "prompt" or "story starter" because a seed grows in all directions — upward mainly, but the roots go down, and offshoots sprout north, south, east, and west. And that's how I want my students' stories to develop.

Using a lame prompt is like planting a seed in stones and expecting it to grow. How can a teacher expect stellar writing when he tells the class to: "Write about what you did during summer vacation." Or, at Thanksgiving time: "Write about what you're thankful for." Or this gem: "Write about your pet." Those same tired prompts were probably used by last year's teacher, and the one before that.

Energize your students with fresh and exciting idea seeds. Change the "pet" prompt to this: "Write a story about a cat, a coconut, and a very angry man." (Kids like writing humorous stories that involve adults being angry or embarrassed.) And when Thanksgiving rolls around, try this idea seed: "Describe the thoughts of a mouse under the table during Thanksgiving dinner."

Not all students in a writing class will take to every idea seed. For some, the "lump of clay" you give them in the beginning of class will remain a "lump of clay" at the end. But every writer has water in the well and it is your job, as the teacher, to tap into it. You must be aware of your students' interests and try to give appealing options.

If your students were in a room full of games, some may sneer at checkers while others avoid Monopoly, or Risk, or Twister, or Scrabble. But everyone will agree to play *something*, right? In the same way, some writers don't enjoy working with fables, but can be easily motivated to write a piece of nonfiction, or an alien adventure, or a romance.

Please remember that your assignments do not always have to begin with the words, "Write a story about..." Instead, try saying "Write..." and insert one of the options from the list below.

> ...a movie review.　　...a travel brochure.　　...a sports report.
> ...a want-ad for a used car or bike.　...a political speech.
> ... an advice column.　　...a weather forecast.

To add interest, challenge your students to write the assignment "as if you were..."

> ...a tired old man.　　　　　...a grumpy bullfrog.
> ...a dainty little princess.　　...an obnoxious comedian.
> ...an irritated grizzly bear.　　...someone very nervous and afraid.

Words of Wisdom (W.O.W.)

Quotations from famous people can make great idea seeds. I call them "Words of Wisdom." Start by writing a quotation on the board, such as:

"It takes a great deal of bravery to stand up to our enemies, but just as much to stand up to our friends." — J.K. Rowling

Students write the quotation, then write their reaction to it. Do they understand what the writer was trying to say? Do they agree with the message? Can they think of a time in their experience when the message applied to them? (If the message is confusing, they may state as much in sentence form.) Have they heard of the person responsible for the quotation? What do they know and how do they feel about the person?

(See Appendix 3 for more Words of Wisdom.)

Writers Switching Roles

As he performs in one movie after another, a Hollywood actor takes on different roles. In one film, he plays the part of a 1930s gangster. In the next, he's a loving father to five children in the Old West. Then he's an anxiety-ridden bank executive in modern-day Wall Street.

In much the same way, a writer often must play different roles. She gets inside the skin of her characters and knows what motivates each one of them — the little boy, the teenaged girl, the professional wrestler, the little old lady, the bus driver, the guy selling hot dogs on the street corner. If she puts a character into her story, she must *be* that character the way an actor portrays a character in a movie.

When she makes that bus driver get angry, how is she going to have him show it? When he laughs, what will it sound like? What does he eat for lunch? When he goes home at the end of the day and learns that his little daughter was naughty at school, what does he say to her? What does he watch on TV? What time does he go to sleep? How does he feel, now that the day is over? The writer should know all this and more.

Try This:

Mix and Match

On the board, write three roles:

A forty-year-old male police officer.
An elderly female librarian.
A teenaged boy who often gets in trouble for lying.

Then write three activities:

Camping.
Grocery shopping.
Bowling.

Randomly assign to each student one of the roles and one of the activities. Students are to write the thoughts of their assigned person doing the assigned activity. For instance, what would that teenaged boy be thinking while he is grocery shopping? What about the librarian bowling?

After a period of time, have each student do the assignment again, this time with a different character doing a different activity. When that is complete, each student will take the role and activity not yet chosen and write the thoughts for that situation.

Tell the class that, in the days ahead, they might be allowed to choose their assignments, or a random selection might be chosen for them. Either way, since they are writers, they will be able to handle it.

Note: When assigning roles, you don't want a student complaining that he's "stuck" with a role he doesn't like, so try to offer choices. ("Pretend you are either a circus clown or a concert pianist...") Consider doing the same with idea seeds. When feasible, offer two to choose from.

For more Idea Seeds, please see *We Think With Ink: The Ideas Book.*

Good Practices

The Difficult Topics Jar

Troubled students don't often walk into class talking openly about what is bothering them. Sometimes, in fact, their insides gnaw away at the bothersome issues all day long without anyone having the slightest idea. The purpose of the Difficult Topics Jar is to spur discussion without drawing attention to or singling out any one member of the class.

A Difficult Topics Jar contains slips of paper, each with a word or phrase addressing a topic that is normally difficult to bring up or discuss.

Draw a slip and read it aloud. ("Divorce.") To help students gather their thoughts on the topic, have them write their definitions of the term. ("When people who are married break up and stop raising a family together.")

Next, tell the students to describe their personal experience in regard to the term. ("My parents almost got a divorce when I was in first grade, but things got better. My uncle got divorced. So did my great-aunt.") If a student has no experience with the topic, have him write a sentence to that effect.

Now have the students write their thoughts on the subject. How do they feel when they hear the word "divorce"? Is divorce sometimes necessary? When a divorce happens, whose fault is it? Is there anything good about a divorce? Is there anything a boy or girl can do to help prevent a divorce in the family? Answers will vary widely and lead to relevant discussion.

Use the Difficult Topics Jar as needed, perhaps as often as once a week. A list of "difficult" topics (not all are appropriate for all grade levels):

divorce	money	jail or prison
the police	homelessness	sickness
greed	anger	no job
death	embarrassment	losing a game
destruction	terrorism	racism
sexism	rude people	disrespect
brothers/sisters	grandparents	vandalism
pollution	cheating	bragging
depression	teasing	cliques
losing a friend	having to move	a fire
a landlord	being ignored	having to share

> *"If you want to change the world,*
> *pick up a pen and write."*
> — *Martin Luther*

Short Lessons

Prior to assigning a new story, you might wish to direct the class's attention to one particular aspect of the language curriculum. Perhaps a "refresher" lesson is in order, brief and focused.

A list of possible topics:

replacing ineffective words with strong ones	organizing/outlining
focusing writing on a particular audience	sequence
using poetic language	changing voice
varying sentence length	using better details
stronger beginnings or endings	eye-catching titles
using humor, exaggeration, or idioms	dialog
using active or vivid words	transitions
cause and effect	punctuation

A different approach: Assign a story and collect the papers, then do one of the short lessons listed above. Return the stories to the students and have them make necessary corrections, focusing on the topic of the short lesson.

(As a way of imparting information about language and writing, consider reading to the class from *We Think With Ink*. Read single paragraphs or sections from Chapters 2, 4, 5, 6, 8, and 9. Discuss and elaborate on what is being read. Many of the topics will trigger lively discussions and may lead to entire lessons.)

Final Thoughts and Suggestions

Team with another class in the school — ideally one from a different grade level — and meet once a week to share written stories.

If at first a shy or underachieving student refrains from reading his story to the class, offer to do the reading for him, or have a friend of his do the honors.

Most fiction includes some factual information, so every writer must do research from time to time. It can be great fun unearthing interesting facts, placing them into a story, and anticipating reader reaction.

Don't waste an opportunity. The street next to the school is being repaved? Go out there and list the sounds and describe the actions. An electrician is in the hall repairing a light fixture? Interview her. Today you had a fire drill? Write about it!

Pound this message into your students: If you are a writer, you must write. A lot. You cannot say you are a writer if, with the same breath, you admit that you haven't written anything in a month. That's like an anteater saying he doesn't eat ants. Or a yellow-bellied sapsucker saying she doesn't suck sap, and that her belly isn't yellow.

Get writing!

Chapter 4

The Building Blocks: Letters, Words, Sentences

Creating a good story is like building a well-made house, with the letters, words, and sentences being the bricks, beams, and walls. Just as a skilled carpenter selects the finest building materials to make a well-crafted home, a writer carefully chooses the perfect words to build the very best sentences in the making of an engaging story. To motivate your students, to make them eager to do creative writing, you must continually point out the interesting aspects of our language, and how the building blocks — the letters, words, and sentences — go together to create all the stories and poems we love so much to read…and to write.

It is important for us writers to know how to use the building blocks. To help your students secure a good grasp on the materials they'll need for the construction of their stories, keep a focus on letters, words, and sentences in your daily routines. As you read together, point out the tricks of the trade that authors use in building their stories and poems. In time, you and your students will become skilled at spotting good — and poor — uses of our language.

Letters

Small children entering the world of reading must first learn the alphabet. After the alphabet is mastered, they plunge into reading words, sentences, and stories. Rarely, if ever, are children told to retrace their steps and analyze the alphabet, but in order to fully grasp the English language, it wouldn't be a bad idea. Let's take some time right now to do just that.

The letters of the alphabet represent the sounds we make with our mouths when we speak and we hear in our minds when we read. About twenty alphabets are used in the world today. The word "alphabet" comes from the first two letters of the Greek alphabet: "alpha" and "beta." The English alphabet has

44

26 letters. The Greek alphabet has 24. There are 33 letters in the Russian alphabet, while the Hebrew alphabet has 22 letters.

The English alphabet certainly has its shortcomings. Our 26 letters are not up to the task of representing all our sounds. For instance, we must put an "s" and an "h" together to make the "sh" sound. Why can't a single letter make that sound? There are other sounds ("ch," "th") that need multiple letters mashed together to produce the results we need. Sometimes the "sh" sound is made with a single "s" ("sugar," "sure") or with "ti"("caution," "lotion"). The letter "c," in "ocean" or "special," can also make the "sh" sound. Confusing, isn't it?

Come to think of it, why does the letter "c" even exist? When we need it for its hard sound ("candy"), we could just use the letter "k," and if we want the soft "c" ("city") we could use "s." Whose silly idea was it to have the letter "c" at all? And what about the letter "x"? We could replace "x" with "ks." Both "tacks" and "tax" would be spelled "taks," and our reading skills would help us to know which is which. For the few words that start with "x," we could use "z" ("zylophone"). So, if we were smart, we would get rid of "c" and "x" and add a letter to make the "sh" sound. These are just a few steps toward improving our alphabet, but don't hold your breath while waiting for changes to happen.

Why do we have the letter "q"? Wouldn't it be easier to spell "quit" with "kw": "kwit"? If there must be a "q," why does a "u" have to follow it almost always? Why in the world are there *any* words that rely on "p" and "h" combined to make the sound of "f" when "f" is right there waiting to be used? Why do we have a hard g ("good") and a soft g ("giraffe"), as well as the separate and distinct "j"? Why not spell all soft "g" sounds with "j" ("jiant," "jemstones," "jymnasium")? When it comes right down to it, couldn't "j" be used in place of "ch"? Who wouldn't understand if you said you went to the store and bought a bag of "potato jips"?

In the books we read and in the stories we write, the consonants used most frequently are "t," "n," "s," and "r." They do the heavy lifting. Less useful are "v" and "z," both of which could be removed from the alphabet completely: "f" could stand in for "v" ("Fictoria from Las Fegas plays the fiolin."), and "s" could take the place of "z" ("Selda's airplane soomed to Sansibar.").

The English alphabet is like a good, but imperfect, symphony orchestra, with more bassoons than are needed and a viola pressed into service to play the parts meant for an absent cello. We writers (conductors) and readers (concert audience) do our best to make do with what we have.

If consonant sounds overlap and cause problems, the vowels are even worse. Consider, for instance, the ever-changing sounds of "o": own, town, top, boat, shoe, foot, boot, from, woman, women, so, to, ouch, touch... What the heck! Try explaining to someone learning our language the difference between "dove" — the bird — and "dove" — the past-tense of dive. (And don't be surprised when she finally understands that and then asks why "dive" became "dove," but "live" doesn't become "love.").

The fact is, our vowels are extremely flexible, changing their sounds from word to word. There are fewer of them — just five (or sometimes six if "y" is used for "i" or "e") out of twenty-six — so each of them is given plenty to do.

Try to read the following passage, from which all the consonants have been removed:

Ue i ae iee eo oei o a iea. ae, ue i aiae i ooa ae a e aiu. e os i ae e o ee a u i. eoe i e a ee ui oo a ei. e ae e, e ae a iie.

No one could make sense of that.

Now read the same passage, this time with the consonants in place, but all the vowels missing:

Stdnts hd scnc lssns cncrnng rcks nd mnrls. Ltr, stdnts prtcptd n ftbll gms t th stdm. Th cch md thm d strtchs nd rn sprnts. Ppl n th stnds wr mnchng ppcrn nd yllng. Whn drknss fll, th gms wr fnshd.

Most people can easily decipher at least 90% of the passage:

Students had science lessons concerning rocks and minerals. Later, students participated in football games at the stadium. The coach made them do stretches and run sprints. People in the stands were munching popcorn and yelling. When darkness fell, the games were finished.

Are the letters of the alphabet able to recreate *all* our worldly sounds? With our mouths, we can try to make the sounds of a truck driving on gravel or of a helicopter racing across the sky. (As all the kids on the playground know, some of us are better than others at making these sounds with our mouths.) Consider this: As a writer, what letters would you assign to the sound of that truck on gravel? Whichever way you do it, your idea isn't likely to match mine ("krkchkchkrch."). It's best to keep the writing of sound effects to a minimum, though if the perfect one is there, go for it. Christopher Morley, in *Parnassus on Wheels*, for instance, nailed the sound of a cow bell: "tonkle-tank."

Onomatopoeia is the formation of a word from the sound it makes. Splash, bang, crackle, whisper, crunch, tinkle, smash, hiss, gurgle, slurp. Pay special attention to what your mouth does when you enunciate the letters in those words. Often the words not only sound like the action being described, but recreate the action with our lips and tongue when we say them. "Boom!" sounds like a bomb exploding, and when we say it, our lips and mouth produce an exploding action.

Try These Letter Games and Activities:

The World of Sounds

Listen for just the consonants made by a truck lumbering past, or a machine digging and grinding into the ground. What vowels do you hear when a lion roars at the zoo, or when a cardinal sits at the top of a tree and calls to all the world?

Listen and Write

Challenge the class to write the letters that spell the sounds you make with your mouth: An unhappy growl: "Aaargh!" A joyful shout at a sports event: "Yaaah!" Now make sounds in other ways. "Crinkle" is an onomatopoetic word we use for the sound of paper being balled up. Ball up a piece of paper and see what your students hear. It might not be "crinkle."

A New Alphabet

Challenge students to make a new alphabet, changing the real letters into new letters they invent. The new letters should include curves and/or straight lines. Each new alphabet should include a key for others to use in deciphering a sentence or an entire message. Variation: Use 15 real letters and 11 that are made up.

Remove a Letter

Write a story. Now remove all the r's (or n's or e's or o's, etc.).
Challenge someone to read your story. How long does it take to realize what
letter is missing?

The NFL Letter Draft

In this game, teams of three or four players choose letters of the
alphabet, taking turns, in the style of the National Football League draft. Pick
until all letters are claimed. Use the letter values from the game of Scrabble:

$1: a, e, i, l, n, o, r, s, t, u
$2: d, g
$3: b, c, m, p
$4: f, h, v, w, y
$5: k
$8: j, x
$10: q, z

While "q" or "z" are worth more than "a" or "t," are used less
frequently, so drafting "a" or "t" might, in the end, result in a higher score.

Volunteers will write the letters of the alphabet on the board and keep a
tally of scores. The teacher, or a chosen student, will read a random passage
from a book, newspaper, or magazine, giving tally marks for the letters as they
are read. The owners of the letters with the greatest point values are the winners.
Allow teams to make trades with each other before starting the next round.

(Have the class imagine what it would be like if they could "own" a
letter of the alphabet and be paid a "royalty" every time the letter is used.)

Words

There are approximately 700,000 words in the English language. If we
include medical and scientific terms, the count goes up to a million. Compare
these numbers to other languages: German: 185,000. Russian: 130,000. French:
not even 100,000. With all our words, we should have no problem expressing
ourselves with precision. Right?

We Think With Ink

As writers (and as speakers) our goal should be to increase our vocabulary daily. The words we use are like tools in a carpenter's toolbox. Even the best carpenter can't do much with just a hammer and a screwdriver. To show his skills he needs a great assortment of tools.

You must remind your students frequently that words have power, weight, and force. Words can be used to do great things, but they also can be hurtful. Words are like stones, some heavy, some light, some sparkly, some dull. Some have sharp edges and can do great damage when thrown recklessly. Words can hurt accidentally, the way a large stone can hurt if dropped by mistake on a toe.

Not all words are created equal. Nouns and verbs are workhorses that carry the load in a piece of writing. If you take a random paragraph and remove everything but the nouns and verbs, the meaning of the paragraph will often still be quite clear. For this reason, writers must choose their nouns and verbs with great care. The nouns and the verbs are the bricks; the adjectives and adverbs, prepositions and articles are the mortar. The bricks, of course, are more important than the mortar.

From crossword puzzles to word games to jokes and riddles, words can be great fun if you know how to play with them.

> *Why did the letter "d" get in trouble?*
> *It made "ma" "mad."*
> *What is the longest word?*
> *Smiles, because there's a mile between*
> *the first and last letters.*
> *What word becomes shorter*
> *after you add two letters to it? Short.*

Someone who doesn't know how to spell, who doesn't know how words work, will not understand these jokes and riddles. The more we know about words and letters, the more we'll understand the jokes and riddles we hear.

We Think With Ink

Try These Word Games and Activities:

Fill in the Blanks

The teacher (or leader) makes a deck of cards with a key word on each. Only she will see the words on the cards. She begins by saying, "I have a four-letter word that starts with 's' and ends with 'p.' What is the word?"

Each student writes a guess. The teacher reveals her word. "The answer I have is 'soap.' What is yours?" Any student who has written "soap" gets three points. Players who have written a different word (snap, stop, soup, etc.) get one point. If a student cannot think of a word with the given letters, he gets no points and will wait for the next example.

Four-, five-, or six-letter words work best for this game. (Try "melt," "past," "again," "first," "soccer," and "packed.")

Category Game

The leader writes three category headings on the board: "Animals," "Things in a Grocery Store," and "Names of Countries." Then he gives the players a list of words. Players are to put the words into the right category. The leader will try to fool the players by including some words that could belong to more than one category ("turkey" could belong to all three of the categories above). The next leader will choose three different categories and provide a different list of words.

Letters into Words

The leader announces, "Make a list of words with 'o-s-t' at the start. Then make a list of words with 'o-s-t' somewhere in the middle. Then make a list of words with 'o-s-t' at the end." When time expires, compare lists. "Ostrich" might be the only word on the first list (sometimes there won't be any), but there will be quite a few on the other two lists: frosting, poster, postpone, ghost, cost, lost, post…

Any 3-letter combinations can be offered. It is good for young thinkers to consider the possibilities, even if in the end there are some lists with no words. Words don't start with 'r-p-e,' but there are many with that 3-letter combination on the inside: carpet, serpent, sharpen, burped, turpentine, warped, and more. Other combinations to try: d-d-l, r-s-t, n-f-l, i-s-t, r-c-h, s-u-m, a-r-p, p-i-c, i-m-p, u-n-n, b-o-t.

Sentences

As teachers, we must demand of our students good, correctly-written sentences. To master the art of sentence writing, young writers need practice, practice, practice. Give your students plenty of opportunities to write. And to read, for we all learn how to be better writers by reading what others have written. Not everything written is written well — it's a mistake to assume a piece of writing is excellent just because a famous author wrote it — so another goal is to become skilled at analyzing what we read.

After your students positively know what a good sentence looks like, show them that the rules of writing can sometimes be broken. (If we don't show them, they are sure to show us. Great literature is filled with "incorrect" sentences.) Breaking language rules can be effective in getting one's point across, in presenting a scene, or establishing mood. Consider the following:

Sheets of rain. Biting wind. Sloshing boots in cold mud. Suddenly, a frantic clopping of horses' hooves, a rickety carriage rolling, jolting, splashing, its wheels spinning and sliding in the deep muddy ruts of Willowby Road.

A strict English teacher might find fault with those sentence fragments, but great literature is filled with examples of skilled authors "breaking the rules." Who is right: the authors or the English teacher?

The Long and Short of It

With most writing, shorter is better than longer. This is too long: "He put on his red shirt. Then he looked in his closet again and saw the blue shirt. He took off the red shirt and put on the blue one. He frowned into the mirror. Should he wear the blue one or the red one? He held the red one up next to the blue one. He wondered what his mom would say. Did the blue shirt go better with the pants he had on? Hmm. Which shirt should he wear?" All that can be replaced with: "He couldn't decide which shirt to wear."

We need to get our readers to the good stuff. "He thought maybe he might decide not to do what he said he was going to do after all." There must be a better, shorter, way of writing that!

Similarly, we should avoid bogging down our stories with unnecessary sentences. "She cracked the egg and let the yolk and the egg white plop into the hot frying pan. While it bubbled and sizzled in the pan, she sprinkled salt and pepper. Using the silver spatula, she flipped the egg, watching the yolk ooze and run to the side of the pan. She placed two pieces of white bread into the toaster and pushed down the mechanism, the dial set on 'dark.' She opened the refrigerator and…"

This story is taking us nowhere in a hurry. Nothing out of the ordinary is happening. We all know what occurs when a person makes a breakfast. We don't have to be told all those details. If nothing important happens until the boy comes down to the breakfast table, we should just write, "She cooked breakfast and waited for Sal to come down to the kitchen."

Try These Sentence Activities:

"Glormpf!"

Give your students this assignment: "Create a sentence not ever written before by anyone in the entire history of the world." The Earth's history goes back a long, long time, so at first this might seem to be an impossible task, but the assignment isn't difficult at all.

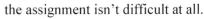

It is enormously easy to put together a sentence no one has ever written before, especially if you use a made-up word in the sentence. Here is one: "When I whacked him on the head, the monster yelled, 'Glormpf!'"

If someone stepped forward with a piece of writing from the 17th century that used those very same words, I could simply add another 'o' or two (or three, or more) to "Glormpf" until I had it. I would then be the first to write that sentence.

52

Sentence Treasure Hunt

Prepare identical decks of word cards for four groups by writing out a long sentence four times, then clipping the individual words to make the decks. (For example, "His homework was very confusing, so he called his friend and asked for help." is a sentence that will result in a deck of 14 cards: "His" "homework" "was" "very" "confusing" "so" "he" "called" "his" "friend" "and" "asked" "for" "help.") Shuffle the cards in each deck. Hand out the decks and ask each group to put the words into alphabetical order.

Set a timer for 15 or 20 minutes. Now challenge the groups to put the words together to make sentences of at least three words. One person in each group records the sentences that are made. Continue making sentences until time is up.

Each sentence of 3 or 4 words = 1 point.
Each sentence of 5 or 6 words = 3 points.
Each sentence of 7 or 8 words = 6 points.
Each sentence of 9 or more words = 12 points.
For one long sentence using all the letters = 20 points.

Other examples: "My cousin and his friend want to come over to play with my new puppy." "Grandma said when she was little, she liked to pretend she was a clown in the circus."

"The true alchemists do not change lead into gold; they change the world into words."
— William H. Gass

Chapter 5

The Power of Words

A high school teacher once wrote the following words at the top of a student's English assignment: "This is absolutely abominable!" The student, not knowing the meaning of "abominable," took it as a compliment and later used the word in a love note to his girlfriend: "I've always wanted to tell you that I think you are abominable."

Nineteenth-century showman P.T. Barnum grew frustrated with people lingering in his museum, preventing new customers from entering. He solved the problem by putting a sign reading "Egress Here" over a door. Thinking they would see something new and exciting in the next room, people learned while standing out in the street that "egress" is simply another word for "exit."

When Satchel Paige first tried out as a professional baseball player, the manager of the Birmingham Black Barons asked him, "Do you throw at that speed consistently?" Paige answered, "No, sir, I do it all the time."

Needless to say, it is important to have a good handle on the words we use every day.

Building a personal vocabulary is every writer's lifelong task. One sure way to increase our vocabulary is to jot down unknown words as we hear them or read them. We record their meanings and pronunciations, and quiz ourselves until we know the words well. When the words become part of our daily vocabulary, we retire them from our list to make room for more unknown words, which are sure to present themselves as we read and listen and live.

In Chapter 4, we compared words in an active vocabulary to tools in a carpenter's tool box and said that just as a builder selects the proper materials and tools, a writer chooses words with great care. It's the words that make or break a story. Words bring scenes to life, drawing the reader into whole new worlds presented on the page.

Often, the perfect word is the one that is most specific. "Collie" is better than "dog." Favor "dash" or "sprint" over "run." Be especially specific with colors and smells. The evening sky wasn't "red," it had "a blush of watermelon." It didn't "smell good" in Grandma's kitchen, my nose was "greeted with an earthy waft of cinnamon and sage."

There are *thousands* of good words from which to choose, words that capture the essence of our subject matter, words that give our mouths a work-out when we say them, words that make us glad we have a voice with which to utter them: lilt, pummel, swish, bobble.

A key element to *We Think With Ink* is to read our writing aloud. By reading aloud, we discover tongue-tangling trip-ups and awkward phrasings. We also uncover parts that stand out for their verbal/aural delicacy and beauty. Even if we read aloud only to ourselves, doing so is a necessary part of not only the revision process, but of the presentation of a finished, polished product. For this reason, we must pay close attention to the sounds of our sentences, and to the sounds of the words themselves.

As a teacher, you must instill in your students a great love for words. You do this by frequently drawing attention to them. Imagine a naturalist guiding a group of students through a forest, stopping often to examine one tree or another, taking a magnifier to the bark, collecting the seeds from the ground, holding the leaves up to the sun. A good teacher will do the same with words as they are being used — written or read — during the course of the day.

Words Can Be Fun to Say

Unveiling a new word to someone is like giving that person a gift. I remember how tickled I was as an adult to learn that, in German, the animal we call a bat is a "fledermaus." Though I can't speak German, I was able to guess that "fleder" means "flying" (not a perfect translation) and "maus" means "mouse." When I was told that "Batman" in German is "Fledermaus Mensch," I couldn't stop saying it over and over. Fledermaus Mensch! Are there other such words and phrases I don't know about yet? I'm sure there are, and I can hardly wait to discover them!

Try This:

Create a "Fun Words" bulletin board. Start with these words and definitions, and invite students to contribute more in the days ahead:

Bamboozle: to deceive.
Exosculate: to kiss loudly.
Kerfuffle: a commotion or fuss.
Skedaddle: to leave quickly or to run away.
Mellifluous: pleasant to hear; musical.
Dolt: a person who is not very smart.
Higgledy-piggledy: confused or jumbled.

Encourage students to use the words in conversation when appropriate. Challenge them to use them at home and then report the family's reaction the next day in class.

When a writer finds a word that is just plain fun to say, she finds a way to get it into her stories. "Splurge" is a good one. So are "jounce" and "squash." "Swift." "Ramshackle." "Sassafras." "Flinch."

Remind your students that beauty is in the eye of the beholder, as well as in the ear of the listener. Just as there are words we like to say, there are others that sound ugly when they roll off the tongue. I'm not talking about words with unpleasant meanings; no one enjoys saying "vomit" or "suffer" because of what these words mean. I mean words like "adapt," which does not have a negative meaning, but to my ears has a bad sound.

The dictionary says a "plot" is a secret plan, or the main events in a book or a movie. To me, "plot" sounds ugly, and the feeling I have has nothing to do with its definition. "Plot" is the sound of a bag of liquidy mush hitting the sidewalk after being dropped from the top of a skyscraper. *PLOT!* The word "truth" represents a good quality, but it sounds unpleasant. The poet John Keats wrote "beauty is truth," but the word "truth" has a displeasing sound to it and isn't fun to say. The same goes for "vouch," "ointment," and "yeast," all words with positive or neutral connotations, but unpleasant to say and hear.

On the other hand, we have some words that are great fun to say even though their meanings are mostly negative: "Monstrosity." "Rambunctious." "Discombobulated."

Alliteration can enhance a piece of writing and be fun to read aloud: "Home, with weeping willows on the weary shore." "He faced the fury of the fiercest among them." Too much alliteration ("Peter Piper picked a peck of pickled peppers...") can become annoying, so writers should use alliteration with caution.

Words can have a rhythmic quality that makes them come alive when spoken out loud. It's no wonder that small children — as well as adults — enjoy the sounds in books like "Chicka-Chicka-Boom-Boom" by Bill Martin, Jr. and John Archambault. And let's not forget the skillful word play in age-old nursery rhymes. Who doesn't love saying "Hickory dickory dock" and "Inty minty tippity fig"?

As writers, we can have a lot of word-fun with our characters' names. Dr. Seuss did it often, and we can too. On a 1940s Jack Benny radio show, comedian Benny refers to the advertising agency of Batten, Barton, Durstine & Osborn. Benny's girlfriend says the name of the agency "sounds like a trunk falling down the stairs." And just try to not repeat after the man who reported that "Ken Dodd's dad's dog's dead."

One Word No One Enjoys Reading Aloud

Nobody ever asks, "How do you spell 'a'?" You also won't hear anyone ask for the spelling of "pneumonoultramicroscopicsilicovolcanokoniosis," but if someone did, you couldn't blame him for wanting help. The fact is, spelling that word is actually rather easy. Break it down and you'll see familiar pieces: pneu (as in "pneumonia") mono, ultra, microscopic, and volcano. The point is, breaking long and difficult words into pieces can make them manageable. ("Pneumonoultramicroscopicsilicovolcanokoniosis," by the way, is a lung disease brought on by inhaling fine silicate or quartz dust. Be careful when you're down in those mines.)

Words Can Be Confusing

Why doesn't "finger" rhyme with "singer"? And why doesn't "finger" or "singer" rhyme with "ginger"? Why don't the last two letters in "derby" match the sound of the last two letters in "nearby"? Shouldn't "surface" start with the same sound as "sure"? Why do "ravel" and "unravel" mean exactly the same thing? What gives the word "colonel" its "r" sound?

It's not just our words that are confusing. Our sentences can be too, especially if we speak unclearly or too quickly. Tell this riddle to your class: "A farmer had twenty sick sheep. One of them died. How many were left?" Most people will think you said "twenty-six sheep" and will give you an answer of 25. They'll be completely befuddled when you tell them the answer is really 19, so repeat the riddle, making sure to mash the words "sick" and "sheep" into each other. When the class starts to say that you're crazy or not very good at subtraction, pretend to be exasperated at their inability to work with numbers and say, "Do I have to write it out for you?" When you write it out and they see *twenty sick sheep* they'll understand the riddle...and how our language can be difficult to understand sometimes.

If I work very hard on Saturday and Sunday, I should speak clearly when I tell people on Monday that the weekend weakened me. I'd better do the same when using the term "natural resources" or someone is sure to hear me say "natural racehorses." And don't even ask about the time I said to my friend, "Get me some ice, would you, please?" I expected him to come back with a glass filled with ice cubes, but he returned instead with a box containing live mice!

When people use our words incorrectly, the confusion is even worse. Some people say "pitcher" when they mean "picture." "I like that pitcher on the wall." *Pitcher on the wall?* A pitcher is either a person who throws a baseball or a large container from which we pour liquid refreshment. "I'm thirsty," you say to your friend. "Would you please bring me a pitcher of water?" "Sure," she says, and a minute later she's handing you a photograph of Niagara Falls.

58

Couldn't They Think of a Different Word?

A building where coins are made is called a mint. A candy flavored with wintergreen, peppermint, or spearmint is also called a mint. One of those two things came first. When the second one came along, why didn't somebody say, "Wait a minute. We already have something called a mint. You'll have to name your new thing something else. 'Rint' hasn't been taken. 'Jint' is also available. How about 'mont' or 'munt' or 'mant'? Please decide on something other than 'mint'." Nope. They couldn't come up with a different combination of letters to make their own unique word. They had to use the same word.

Imagine how confusing it must be for someone learning our language, hearing that a mine is a place where gold is dug from the ground, only to learn a little later that "mine" is also the opposite of "yours." And what about the word "fine"? A sign that says "Fine for Parking Here" could be taken as permission to do so. Is it really okay, or will you get in trouble for parking your car there?

Most people know the word "safety" refers to the state of being safe and out of danger. In football, a "safety" is a player on defense positioned behind the linebackers. Even crazier, in football a "safety" also means a play in which the quarterback is tackled in the end zone. Come on. They couldn't think of a different word? In baseball, it's even more of a puzzle: A "ball" is the round object being hit and thrown and caught. A "ball" is also a pitch not over the plate. And after the game, one of the players could very well say, "We had a ball at the game today," meaning they had a lot of fun.

"Pretty" means "nice looking," as in "What a pretty smile you have." "Pretty" can also mean "kind of," as in "I was pretty mad at him." So, is "a pretty little puppy" a good-looking puppy or one that is rather small?

Is "plant" the best name they could think of for a place of industry and manufacturing? Really? The word "wound" has two different meanings and is pronounced two different ways. For an injury to the skin, why couldn't they just have gone with "owwie"?

"Medium" is the size between small and large. Why couldn't they leave "medium" alone and find a more exciting word for the person who can relay messages from the spirit world? (By the way, did you know that mediums almost never receive compliments? Even after a successful séance, it is *rare* for a *medium* to hear, *"Well done."*)

> *I wonder what the kumquat, peach, and apricot*
> *had to say when they first heard about their cousin,*
> *the "orange." The wordsmiths must have been*
> *extremely lazy the day they named that fruit.*
> *At least they didn't continue with the trend —*
> *we don't call cherries "reds" and blueberries "blues."*

A "date" is a romantic meeting between two people *and* a kind of fruit, which leads to the story of a man on his 50th wedding anniversary saying that it all started at the farmer's market when he innocently said to the young woman, "I'd like to have a date with you." And then there's the one about the baseball player who told his friend, "The ball hit me and made my arm smart," to which the friend said, "Too bad it didn't hit you on the head."

Perhaps the most annoying double use of a single word is "ear," as in an "ear of corn." What? And how about the word "relish," which takes us to such sentences as: "I'm going to eat this hot dog with relish."

I guess we really should be thankful that so many words have double meanings. Without them, imagine how thin all the joke books would be.

Words Can Be Invented

There are 700,000 words in the English language, but that isn't enough. We need more because sometimes we come to a crossroads in our writing and the perfect word isn't there for us. One option is to use "whatchamacallit," "thingamajig," "whatchamajiggy," "thingamabob," "doohickey," "wheezit," "oojah," "thingy," or "whatnot." Or we can make up a word of our own. If we do it right, our readers won't object.

In Kenneth Grahame's *The Wind in the Willows*, the character Mole "scraped and scratched and scrabbled and scrooged" through the soil until he popped up into the daylight.

In her comic strip *For Better or For Worse,* Lynn Johnston has a dog making these perfect sounds as he drinks from a dish on the floor: "Galoorp! Gaslurp! Slupp!"

In the song "Sun King" by the Beatles, John Lennon wrote lyrics that make no sense, but sound quite nice anyway:

We Think With Ink

"Quando paramucho mi amore de felice carathon.
Mundo paparazzi mi amore cicce Verdi parasol.
Questo abrigado tantamucho que canite carousel."

In the following poem, there are so many nonsense words that by the
last line, when we read the real word "bobolink," it sounds like one of the
nonsense words. Read this one aloud, if you dare.

The Bobolink
The bobolink bobbled his brug brimmodaire
And frabbled his fungo-ozwando;
He spazzled and chuggaed his lyg miffligaire
While pandigging out his frassmando.
His mushig, however, galog on the siller
And quinsagged his plag into mink
But the ginzook cowldiggered and piggled the briller
'Twas the flob sol of our bobolink.
—Anonymous

"Chargoggagomanchaugagochaubunagungamaug" is the name of a lake
in Massachusetts. Somebody put those letters together and made that word,
thinking it was just the perfect word for that lake. It's an Indian word that
means: "You fish on that side, we'll fish on this side, and nobody will fish in the
middle."

Some individuals have made up words that eventually found their way
into the dictionary. William Shakespeare is given credit for inventing "scuffle,"
"newfangled," "eyeball," "cold-blooded," "bedazzled," and many others. Mark
Twain gave us "blip," "lunkhead," "slumgullion," and "hard-boiled." From
Lewis Carroll, we got "galumph," "chortle," and more. And don't forget Teddy
Roosevelt, who famously coined "pussyfoot" and "mollycoddle."

Cartoonist H. T. Webster gave us a meek character named Caspar
Milquetoast; now "milquetoast," meaning "a timid individual," is in the
dictionary. If you're grumpy at Christmas time, someone might accuse you of
being a "Scrooge" or a "Grinch," both characters from the imaginations of
fiction writers (Dickens and Seuss), and now terms we use as everyday words.
The champion of made-up words has to be Richard and Robert Sherman's

"supercalifragilisticexpialidocious," a word put together to make an amusing song sound just right.

Wouldn't it be nice to be clever enough to invent a word that people enjoy so much that they make it a part of their working vocabulary?

Some Thoughts About Nouns, Verbs, Adjectives, Adverbs...and Pronouns

The following passage, from Hamlin Garland's *A Son of the Middle Border*, describes a winter storm on the open prairie c. 1870. Notice how Garland uses nouns and verbs to bring the experience to life.

...the blasts...swept down over the plain to hammer upon our desolate little cabin and pile the drifts around our sheds and granaries...Hour after hour those winds and snows in furious battle howled and roared and whistled around our frail shelter, slashing at the windows and piping on the chimney...On the third morning, we thawed holes in the thickened rime of the window panes and looked forth on a world silent as a marble sea and flaming with sunlight...the yard was piled high with drifts and the barns were almost lost to view...

The adjectives aren't bad: desolate, furious, frail, thickened, silent. But it is the nouns (blasts, drifts, winds, snows, rime of the window panes, marble sea) and the verbs (swept, hammer, howled, roared, whistled, slashing, piping, flaming) that allow us to know — to feel — what it was like for Garland and his family to hunker down in a rustic cabin during a brutal winter storm.

Nouns and Adjectives

Nouns are facts and adjectives are opinions. Either the grizzly bear lumbered into the campsite or it didn't. Saying that a bear was there is stating a fact. Describing the grizzly as "gigantic" is an opinion. "Gigantic" compared to what? Compared to the little kid in the tent? Compared to another grizzly bear?

The nouns you use are easy to verify; the adjectives are not. If a **man** is sitting in a **car**, we know those things; they are facts. If adjectives are involved, now we have opinions. One person might see a **nice** man sitting in a **flashy** car; someone else sees a **creepy** man sitting in an **ugly** car.

Adjectives are often completely unnecessary. If a boy is picking up a pile of doggy doo-doo in the yard, we don't have to write: "He winced at the unpleasant odor." That extra information is annoying. No one has to be told that the odor of doggy doo-doo is "unpleasant." Removing that word will make the sentence simpler, clearer, better. Respect the reader's intelligence; allow him to put two and two together for himself.

When a writer uses an adjective, she is inserting her opinion into the story, often without even knowing she's doing it. And the story is weaker because of it. Clifton Fadiman called the adjective "the banana peel of the parts of speech." Be careful with adjectives.

There are times, however, when an adjective is just what a writer needs to present the perfect picture. We don't have many synonyms for "headache," so if we're trying to describe an especially painful one, we may need an adjective. Which of these paints the better picture and will earn you more sympathy:

"I have a bad headache."

"I have a skull-crushing headache."

Verbs and Adverbs

If the individual words in a seven-word sentence could be lined up as if they were human beings, the verb would be the outgoing one, the one that's full of energy, the one with ideas and drive, the leader of the group. A sentence with a weak verb is like a group of people with no true leader, a group that isn't doing anything of consequence or going anywhere in particular.

A good verb is always better than a weak one bolstered by adverbs. Compare these two sentences:

"I'm going to get you," he said playfully.

"I'm going to get you," he teased.

"Teased," of course, is better than "said," even if "said" is helped by "playfully." And please don't try to strengthen an already strong word with an adverb. Because the word "tease" implies playfulness, "he teased playfully" is just not good. The same applies to "he growled angrily" or "he giggled happily."

If you're describing a man being questioned by the police, you might write, "He bit his lip nervously." Do you need "nervously"? The situation and the verb provide all the clues that are needed. The reader knows that someone biting his lip in a police station is *nervous*. Try to remember that most sentences are better with fewer words. And try to avoid using words ending with "-ly."

A good verb *shows* the reader what is happening in the story. Compare:

"He walked very slowly and quietly."
"He tiptoed."

Don't *tell* the reader everything. Allow her to figure out, from the word "tiptoe," that the character was walking slowly and quietly.

"He was really cold."
"He shivered."

In the first sentence, the verb is "was." Very weak. In the second, the verb is "shivered." In the second sentence, the writer avoided injecting his opinion with an adjective. The first sentence *tells* the reader that the character was cold. "He shivered" *shows* it.

Pronouns

Pronouns stand in for nouns, the way "he" stands in for "George Washington" in the following passage: "George Washington glared at the men. Then he jumped on his horse and rode off to the west." There is no confusion; the reader knows that "he" is "George Washington." Some sentences, however, are written less carefully, leaving the reader wondering who exactly "he" or "she" or "it" is. Can you see the problems in the following sentences?

1. My father watched the elephant do tricks at the circus, then he was taken outside and fed 20 pounds of hay.

2. A message to parents: Anger and frustration are not good for your children, so do your best to get rid of them.

3. The batter hit the baseball off the pitcher's leg. It then rolled to the shortstop.

4. Please don't tie your dogs to the trees because they might bark and disturb the neighbors.

5. My brother noticed a wart on his leg, so he had it removed.

6. Her grandmother died when she was only six years old.

7. "There was a farmer who had a dog and Bingo was his name-o..." Was Bingo the dog's name or the farmer's?

Try These:

Revised Nursery Rhymes

Take a famous nursery rhyme that uses nonsense words (Diddle diddle dumpling, Hickory dickory dock, Home again home again jiggity-jig, etc.) and change the nonsense words into nonsense words of your own.

Alternative: Take a familiar melody (London Bridges, Skip to My Lou, Sing a Song of Sixpence, etc.) and rewrite the words with nonsense syllables.

Do You Know What it Means?

Challenge your students to use vocabulary words to make jokes involving the word meanings:

What does "procrastination" mean? I'll tell you tomorrow.

What does "insomnia" mean? I couldn't sleep a wink last night, so I'm just too tired to tell you.

What does "stubborn" mean? I won't tell you. Come on, tell me. No!

A Confusing Poem

Write a rhyming poem drawing from the following list of words. Have a partner read the poem aloud. She will have to think quickly to decide if "bow," for instance, should sound like "brow" or "blow."

doe	foe	hoe	Joe	Edgar Allan Poe			shoe	toe
woe	achoo	bamboo	boo	goo	moo	too	zoo	blow
bow	brow	chow	cow	crow	flow	glow	how	know
low	meow	Moscow	now	plow	row	sow	tow	vow
wow	blew	brew	dew	few	flew	grew	knew	new
sew	stew	view	blue	cue	clue	due	glue	hue
sue	Sue	bough	cough	dough	enough	tough	though	through
do	Flo	go	no	so	to	two	who	bluff
fluff	gruff	stuff	flu	gnu	Lulu	Stu	Lou	you

Chapter 6

The Making of a Story, Article, or Poem

When I was a boy, every December my family would gather in the kitchen to make Christmas cookies. Mom would roll the dough, and we kids chose cookie cutters for the shapes we wanted: snowman, star, bell, etc. After the cookies had baked, we slathered them with frosting: white, green, or red, or a combination of different colors. Then we decorated the cookies with sprinkles and jimmies and candies. Some liked the frosting thick, some thin. Some loaded on the jimmies, some were satisfied with a small amount. Each cookie we created was unique.

The ingredients were the same, just put together differently.

We make stories in class the same way. We start with the same directions: "Write a story about a boy who gets into trouble with his mother, but does something in the end that makes her smile." In one person's story, the boy is named Brandon. He makes a big mess in the living room. His mother is having friends over and is upset about the condition of the living room. The next writer's main character is named Alex, and he comes home late from school and doesn't have time for his chores. The next writer doesn't give his boy a name, but has him breaking a lamp in his bedroom. Each story is made with the same "ingredients" — the words in the dictionary — but are selected by individual writers with ideas all their own. And each story goes off in its own direction.

In a class where students' writing is shared and critiqued, individual styles will develop and become familiar to all. Stories have personalities just like people, and, with time, we will recognize the writing styles of the others in class. Compare story-writing to cookie-making: You know the cookie with pink frosting belongs to your friend Mary because her favorite color is pink; the one loaded with hot cinnamon candies must be Brian's because that's his style.

In the same way, we recognize our friends' ways with words. Mary's love for animals comes through in her stories. We've also come to expect her to use short words and choppy sentences. Brian, on the other hand, has a great interest in sports. He flavors his stories with references to full court presses and all-out blitzes. He also prefers rambling sentences with words that are full of action, like "collision" and "explosion."

Remember: After reading books, poems, and magazine articles, it's a natural step for someone to want to write her own books, poems, and magazine articles. But writing is not easy. Stories, poems, and articles are not Christmas cut-out cookies. There isn't a set recipe to follow that will produce a predictably satisfying product in the end. The pieces come not from a cupboard, but from the writers' imaginations and talents.

> *"What an astonishing thing a book is.*
> *It's a flat object made from a tree with*
> *flexible parts on which are imprinted*
> *lots of funny dark squiggles. But one*
> *glance at it and you're inside the mind*
> *of another person, maybe somebody dead*
> *for thousands of years. Across the millennia,*
> *an author is speaking clearly and silently*
> *inside your head, directly to you."*
> — *Carl Sagan*

A good way to begin your writing instruction is to **write a story together with your class**. To do this effectively, you, the teacher, must be able to think on your feet and be quite creative on the spot, so you might want to practice a bit before attempting this activity.

Start by saying, "One day a girl went for a walk in the woods all by herself. The girl's name was…" Point to one of the students and wait for him to supply the name. Then continue with the story. "…Carly. Well, it was a beautiful summer afternoon and Carly was really enjoying herself. She walked down a path lined with daisies and sunflowers, and she kept going until she found herself at the top of a high hill. That's when she saw a big group of…" Point to someone different who will fill in this blank. "…foxes. And there were how many of them?" Point. "Six. Well, Carly stood there watching the six foxes as they jumped and played in the grass…"

Take the story anywhere you want it to go. Be warned that students' contributions often get more and more ridiculous. If one of them wants there to be a group of hippopotamuses on that hilltop, so be it. "Six hippopotamuses escaped from the zoo that morning and…"

There's room for humor in creating a story this way. Once I motioned to a girl, expecting her to tell us what Carly said at a crucial point in the story and, suddenly on the spot, she couldn't think of anything. She nervously said, "Um…" and I ran with it. "Carly said, 'Um,' and the foxes ran and jumped right over her." Later in the story I had Carly telling her mother about her experience. "Then the foxes started running after me. I said, 'Um,' and they jumped right over me!" The class laughed every time the "Um" line was repeated.

Once the story is complete, go back over the events and write the story together on the board for all to see. Here is where you demonstrate how a writer thinks and works. As you write the story, model how a writer chooses words, elaborates, edits, and organizes. Think out loud as you formulate the paragraphs, commenting on indentation, spelling, and other factors as you go.

> *"I could never have dreamt that there were such goings-on in the world between the covers of books, such sandstorms and ice blasts of words, such staggering peace, such enormous laughter, such and so many blinding bright lights, splashing all over the pages."*
> *— Dylan Thomas*

Getting Started

Before your students begin a new story, draw their attention to these three questions: 1) Who is my audience? 2) What is my point of view? 3) What will the title be?

Who is My Audience?

When we are writing (or speaking), to have effective communication, we must know our audience. As we write, we think of who will be reading our story, and we write it with that person (or those people) in mind. **With different audiences, we change the words we use and the way we put them together.** Imagine a high school student going over the rules of a new game with a classmate. Now imagine that same person explaining the rules of the game to a 3-year-old child. He adjusts his language to fit his audience.

If a girl is writing an article for the sports page of a newspaper, she might write: *He tore into the split-finger fastball with his trusty Louisville Slugger, sending the horse hide sphere 400 feet to the warning track and beyond, over the fence, into the stands for a grand slam home run.* If she's writing for a children's magazine, she'd be wise to shorten it to: *He hit the ball high into the air. Up, up, up...a home run!*

When one ornithologist (bird expert) writes to another, she might say something about the morning sunshine being "the color of a carduelis tristis," but most people would understand her better if she were less scientific and simply wrote that it was "the color of a gold finch." The first example is technically correct, but if the reader doesn't understand what is written, successful communication is not happening.

Think of it this way: Children's picture books are not written by little children; they're written by adults who know their audience and use language that is right for them.

A middle school student might write a message to a friend that says: *What U doin at 4?* We can assume that if the audience were his grandmother, the student would phrase the message differently: *What are you going to be doing today at four o'clock, Grandma?*

How a person writes what he writes depends on his audience. In the old days, a writer might have said, "Your presence is requested at the dinner party of Madam Wentworth on the evening of March 19 in the year of the Lord 1845." Most would now write, "Please join us for dinner next Saturday. 5-ish." A texter would say, "U wanna eat? Sat. at 5."

What's the Point...of View?

All stories are told from a point of view. Who is telling the story? From what position? A Fourth of July parade will be described differently by two people standing on opposite sides of Main Street. Not only will they see the parade from different angles, their attitudes will be different. They will experience (and describe) *two different parades.*

The parade could be seen from many points of view. A writer at the start of the parade route would see marchers, musicians, and clowns full of energy and excitement, while one near the end would find the participants drooping and worn. A writer could describe the parade from the point of view of someone *in* the parade – the tuba player, the mayor giving a shake to anyone extending a hand, the little Girl Scout trying desperately to keep up with the troop.

Once the point of view is established, the writer can decide on a voice to use. For instance, one writer might tell the story of the parade the way a child would see it, while another tells it in the voice of a doctor or a football coach, a garbage man or a college professor.

> *Different voices saying the exact same thing:*
> *Old lady: "In all my born days, I've never*
> *seen the likes of such a thing."*
> *Young man #1: "That's a first for me."*
> *Young man #2: "I, like, you know, never saw*
> *nothing like that, like, ever before."*

A writer might pretend to be a bird looking down at the parade from a nest high in an oak tree, or a cat half asleep in the window on the third floor of an apartment building, or a squirrel who keeps dashing from one side of the street to the other. In the hands of a good writer, the story could even be told by an inanimate object. One of the sticks in the hands of the drummer in the

71

marching band would have an interesting story to tell. So would the popsicle being eaten by that boy in his mother's lap. Or the fire hydrant made nervous by all the dogs attending the festivities.

Same parade, different points of view, different voices.

For any story, the writer must decide who is doing the telling and from what point of view. Is it a straight narrator, in third person, using words like "he," "she," "they"? ("Laura trudged all the way home in the rain, too angry to notice her soaked shoes.") Or is the main character telling the story in first person, using "I," "me," "we"? ("I was never so mad in my life. I could hardly see through the pouring rain as I plodded through the puddles on Wilton Road.") Or is a side character telling the story in first person? ("Laura walked ahead of me, storming into the sheets of rain. I called to her over and over, and she kept ignoring me.") A single story told from three different angles and in three different voices.

> *Good writing begins with good old-fashioned English sentences that are grammatically correct. Once we are able to express ourselves in straight language, we then can take paths off that main road into the world of using the voices of others: a small child, a naughty puppy, or an angry old man.*

Sometimes if a story is not clicking, the writer can try changing the point of view. Someone else can tell the story, using a different voice and a different understanding. To drive home the idea of how to do this, read "Goldilocks and the Three Bears" to your students. Most versions of the story are told by a narrator in third person. Challenge your students to tell the same story from a different point of view. How would Mama Bear tell the story? Would she tell it with humor? Or would she be angry? Or worried and nervous? Try it with Goldilocks doing the narrating. Or have the third bowl of porridge give its version of the story. Or the first chair that broke. Or Baby Bear's comfy bed.

Try These:

Switching Voices

Write a story. Now write it again in the voice of:

your favorite cousin.   your best friend.   your father.
your grandmother.   your dog/pet.   someone famous.

Topic and Voice Cards

Make a deck of "Topic" cards:

What is your favorite holiday?
How do you feel on Christmas Eve?
How do you feel about your oldest relative?
How do you feel about weekends?
How do you feel about Mondays?
Describe your house.
Describe a big, busy meal at a restaurant.
Describe a traffic jam.
I get horribly sad when I think of…
Something that scares me is…
The time of day I do not like is…
Describe a poor person.
Describe someone with lots of money.
Describe someone who just went to a funeral.
How does holding a little baby make you feel?

Make a deck of "Voice" cards:

A 99-year-old man.   A teacher you know.
A well-known cartoon character.   Your grandmother.
Your next-door neighbor.   A truck driver.
A two-year-old girl.   A manatee.

George Washington.	A cow.
An enormous giant.	A pirate.
Someone dying of thirst on the desert.	A tiny tree frog.
A professional football player.	A ghost.
A guitar player in a rock band.	The school principal.

Each student draws two "Topic" cards and two "Voice" cards. He chooses one of the two voices and uses it to write about one of the two topics he has chosen. (Using two cards from each deck allows the students to make choices.)

Choosing a Good Title

Often, the difference between a story that draws the interest of readers and one that is ignored is the title. Readers make quick decisions, and they pass over perfectly good stories because the titles aren't exciting or interesting or adventurous or humorous enough.

Some writers know their story's title before a single word is written. Others wait until the story is finished, then take days to decide on a title, changing it several times in the process. Katherine Anne Porter said, "I always write my last line, my last paragraphs, my last page first." Not all writers operate that way. In fact, most writers will admit to being inconsistent, sometimes knowing titles and endings from the get-go, and other times not.

> *When you're writing a story, don't let the title hold you up. Plow ahead. Write. A good title will come to you...most likely.*

Try These:

Guess the Title

Without telling the title, read a short story aloud. Have the class brainstorm good titles for the story. Discuss strengths and weaknesses of the suggested titles. Reveal the actual title. Discuss. Is the title a good one? Are any of the titles suggested by the class better than the real one?

> *Play for the class Beethoven's "Moonlight Sonata."*
> *Ask the class to listen for clues as*
> *to why this is a good title. Discuss.*
> *Tell the class that the real title is "Piano*
> *Sonata No. 14 in C Sharp Minor, Opus 27,*
> *No. 2," and that Beethoven himself had*
> *attributed the emotion of the piece to sitting*
> *at the bedside of a friend who had suffered*
> *an untimely death. Inform the class*
> *that in 1832, five years after Beethoven*
> *died, a music critic compared the sonata*
> *to the effect of moonlight shining on Lake*
> *Lucerne, and the interpretation became*
> *so popular that by the end of the century*
> *most people had forgotten the real title.*

Critique the Cover

Select a number of library books for analysis. Show the cover of the first book. Is the title good? What about the cover art and design? Discuss what makes an attractive cover. Remind the students that they will be making booklets in class and that they will be the designers of the covers for those booklets.

Rate the Titles

What is good about each of these titles? What is not so good? Discuss.

The Polar Bear and the Frog
A Cup of Monster Blood
How My Little Brother Saved the World

We Think With Ink

The Worst Day Ever
The Cute Little Puppy
A Really Big Thing
Why the Clown Left the Circus
Forest Fire!
The Christmas Present Mystery
The Sun Was Hot
The Day My Grandmother Took Me Fishing
I Was Abraham Lincoln's Childhood Friend
The Night We Thought We Heard a Ghost, but It was Only the Wind in the
Trees

(Add more to this list as you come upon good or not-so-good titles.)

Chapter 7

Games: An Essential Piece of the Puzzle

Games are a serious part of *We Think With Ink*. In the playing of games, concepts sink in and stay with learners. Word games and language-related puzzles fully immerse players in the language. Days after playing a word game, connections click in the brain of a player while he's reading or listening.

Many of the classroom games described below work well because they involve all students actively thinking, building on each other's ideas, making connections together as a group. With most games, a sense of competition is essential, but players in the classroom must be made aware that **everyone is winning when learning is happening**. Knowledge has a magic quality: when one person shares it with others, all now have it. When we play a word game as a class, even the losers always win.

Envision a scene where all students are thinking, clamoring for a solution. One student finally produces the answer. You ask the student, "How did you do it?" and the answer is analyzed so everyone understands. In the end, you have one proud student feeling very good about herself, and everyone else in the class satisfied and happy, too.

In my classroom, the puzzles and games were usually saved for Friday as a reward for hard work throughout the week. I would introduce a new type of puzzle and use variations of it over the next few weeks. After the students became familiar with the rules of one puzzle, new puzzles and games were introduced. As the school year progressed, a comfortable mix of the familiar and the new was continually employed.

We teachers can make use of existing games (board games, TV game shows, word puzzles in newspapers or magazines) and tailor them to fit the lessons being taught in class. Teacher-created word puzzles and games take time and energy to produce, but, once made, become part of the teacher's repertoire.

Some of the games described below must be led by the teacher. Others are played by the students independently. Some of the games work best with students grouped in teams, competing with other teams. The teams can be small (3 or 4 per team) or large (one half of the class against the other). The best games often require students to be out of their seats, putting their heads together and figuring out solutions with teammates.

Many of the games require preparation, such as the making of game pieces or decks of cards. Students can be called on to do the constructing. In my classroom, the games were often made one day and played the next. Because the students must sometimes research information for the cards or for the boards used in the games, much learning happens during the making of the games. There is a special kind of camaraderie on display in a room where students are competing at games devised and created by classmates.

Five by Five

Each player starts with a game sheet of five rows and five columns. (Depending on need, other configurations may be employed.)

At the top of each column, write a subject. For instance: "Five-letter Verbs," "Synonyms for 'Big,'" "Famous Scientists," "Cities in Our State," "A Brand of Cereal." (To enhance the interest for my students, I often included a category not related to the class work.)

Choose letters to be written on the left, one for each row. Let's say: "L," "R," "E," "S," and "D." (Avoid "X" and other letters that might be difficult.) In a set amount of time, the boxes are to be filled appropriately. Example: Answers across the "E" row might be "enter," "enormous," "Einstein," "East Troy" and...hmmm, I can't think of a cereal that starts with "E." It's okay for that to happen. Leave that box blank and better luck next time.

We Think With Ink

The game sheet below shows the results of a typical game.

	5-letter nouns	3-letter verbs	Adjectives used at the Beach	Famous Author	Brand of Candy
S	shell	spy	salty	Seuss	Snickers
D	drink	dig		Dickens	Dum-Dums
R	ranch	run	rough	Rowling	Reese's
O	organ				~~Oreo~~
H	hiker	hop	hot		Hershey's

Players should not expect to always fill the board completely. If answers do not come to mind, the spaces are left blank. The teacher will judge if the answers fit the category. Since "Oreo" is considered a cookie, not a candy, no points were given for that answer. Players are not penalized for incorrect answers, so encourage your students to fill in as many boxes as possible.

Scoring: Each player marks the correct answers, then squares the numbers of correct answers going across each row, and those going down each column. There were 5 correct answers for the "S" words going across, so that row is worth 5 x 5, 25. Same for the "R" row. The "O" row had just 1 correct answer, so the row was worth 1 point (1 x 1 = 1). The "D" and "H" rows had four good answers each and 4 x 4 = 16, bringing the totals for the rows of this score sheet to 25 + 16 + 25 + 1 + 16 = 83. Doing the same for the columns under the subject titles, we find scores of 25 + 16 + 9 + 9 + 16 = 75. The total score, then, is 83 + 75 = 158. Not bad.

Word Jumbles and Crypto-messages

Word Jumbles and Crypto-messages can be found on-line, in newspapers, or in puzzle books and magazines. They usually feature plays on words involving puns. If your students are not acquainted with these puzzles, demonstrate how to work them by doing examples at the board, thinking aloud as you go. As the students begin to understand, rely on them to do some of the thinking and figuring as you work the puzzles together. Eventually, they will be able to do the puzzles themselves.

Word Jumbles

Word Jumbles help us to see how letters go together to form words. When we see "WRNAD," we notice different ways the letters might go together. In some words, such as "dwarf," we see "D" and "W" next to each other, but that is rare. Will we see "R" followed by "W" in a 5-letter word? Not often, if at all. So we try combining the letters in different ways, knowing that some combinations are not likely.

For most five-letter words that have just one vowel, the vowel will be in the very middle. Hmmm. "D" and "R" might start the word, and — yes! The word is "DRAWN."

To demonstrate a Word Jumble, start by writing a riddle question on the board. Let's use the riddle from page 49 of this book. "What word becomes shorter after two letters are added to it?"

Now draw the number of blanks in the answer. "__ __ __ __ __" Then write out the clues, which are four words with their letters jumbled, followed by blanks. The underlined blanks indicate letters used to spell out the answer to the riddle.

> "mils O O O O   actr O O O O
> chit O O O O   wrob O O O O"

The students will work at unscrambling the four-letter words: "SLIM, CART, ITCH, and BROW." The underlined letters, S, R, T, H, and O are now to be unscrambled to give the answer to the riddle: "What word becomes shorter when you add two letters to it?" "SHORT."

I made the Word Jumbles below from riddles found in a joke book. Puzzles like these are not hard to construct yourself. Your students could also try to make them. Be careful, however. The letters of some words, when scrambled, can be unscrambled to make entirely new words — the letters of "draw" are the same as those in "ward," those in "time" are also in "item," the same letters in "taste" go into "state," etc. — and the letters you expect a player to use to solve your riddle are not the letters they will be using, making your puzzle hopelessly confusing and unsolvable.

We Think With Ink

What kind of bears live at the North Pole?

— — — —   — — — —

ild   O O O   yonp O O O O

vone O O O O   shac   O O O O

Answers: l i d   p o n y   o v e n   c a s h

COLD ONES

What flowers do all people have?   — — — — — —

yast O O O O   noud O O O O

lipa O O O O   nico O O O O

Answers: s t a y   u n d o   p a i l   c o i n

TULIPS (two lips)

We learn much about words and language when doing Word Jumbles. We analyze how words are made, and are required to determine which words are possible with certain letter combinations (" __ __ o y" could be "ploy," "ahoy," "buoy," etc.).

Even if we fail to complete a puzzle, when we are shown the solution, we learn and will likely do better the next time. Once your students become acquainted with Word Jumbles, don't be surprised if they offer to make some for the class. That is exactly what you want, because making puzzles broadens our grasp on the language even more than solving puzzles. And don't forget: Homemade word puzzles can be good for introducing or reinforcing concepts and information learned in the general curriculum.

Crypto-messages

As with Word Jumbles, Crypto-messages help us to see how letters go together to form words. In a Crypto-message, each letter of the alphabet is substituted with another letter. Using the substituted letters, a message — often one involving a play on words — is written. Players are to decipher the message by determining which letters have been substituted.

The best way to explain how to solve a Crypto-message is to work on one together as a group. Here is a Crypto-message I once made for my class:

JA   VEF   YJKTVFFAVE   JY   HQTME,

HQVE   BVKWFAVB   MFXFZTQVF   DN   WQO.

Crypto-message puzzles usually come with a clue. For this puzzle, the clue is: V = T. So, players start by replacing all the V's with T's:

JA   TEF   YJKTTFFATE   JY   HQTME,

HQTE   BTKWFATB   MFXFZTQTF   DN   WQO.

The second word has three letters, the first being a "T." Supposing the word to be "THE," players will change all the E's to H's and all the F's to E's.

JA   **THE**   YJKTTEEATH   JY   HQTMH,

HQTH   BTKWFATB   MEXEZTQTE   DN   WQO.

What two-letter word could start the sentence? Whatever it is, the fourth word in the message starts with the same letter and has just two letters as well. "IF" and "IS"? "ON" and "OF"? Players can try one pair or the other and see what happens. Let's say they try "ON" and "OF":

ON   **THE**   **FO**KTTEENTH   **OF**   HQTMH,

HQTH   BTKWFNTB   MEXEZTQTE   DN   WQO.

82

The third word is almost complete and is seen to be "FOURTEENTH." Now the players know that K = U and T = R. They use that information to fill in the corresponding letters elsewhere, which helps them to complete another word, which leads to another, and another, until they figure out the message:

"ON THE FOURTEENTH OF MARCH, MATH STUDENTS CELEBRATE PI DAY."

Care must be taken when solving Crypto-messages. If we see "__ F T E __," we might assume that the word is "AFTER." We make the corresponding changes and start wrestling around in confusion until we realize that the word in question was "OFTEN." We must use context clues and other reading strategies to be sure the message in the puzzle makes sense.

An experienced player will begin to spot dependable clues and tricks that present themselves in most of these puzzles. Here are a few to consider:

If there is an apostrophe before the last blank, the last letter is most likely "S" (if the word is a possessive) or "T" (if the word is a contraction). If it indeed is "T," then the letter before it is "N."

If there is a question mark at the end of the sentence, the first word will probably be "WHAT" or "HOW" or another of the words that begin question sentences.

If a word contains the letter "I" positioned third from the end, it could mean that the word ends with "ING." The same applies if "N" is found second from the end, or if "G" is found at the end of a word.

If a quick scan finds a four-letter word that begins and ends with the same letter, the word, most likely, is "THAT." But be careful. It could be "ELSE," "SETS," "TENT," or a similar word.

With more experience, more such clues will be evident.

TV Game Shows

Popular TV game shows can be reformulated into instructional games for the classroom. While electronic versions of some of the shows are available, creating game boards and playing pieces as a group is, in my mind, the better approach. The teacher, at first, will devise the questions and answers. Later, the students themselves can volunteer to create the challenges.

Consider recreating "Jeopardy!" or "Wheel of Fortune" for classroom use. A "Jeopardy!" game board can be created from cardboard, construction paper, and 3x5 cards. Categories can cover curriculum-related topics (7-Letter Nouns, Rules of Grammar, Science Terms, Presidents). As in the TV show, answers are written for which questions are to be provided.

The hardest part about playing "Wheel of Fortune" in the classroom is the making of a serviceable spinning wheel, but you can manage with something simple. (Resourceful students will sometimes rise to the challenge of constructing a good spinning wheel. Or perhaps you'll be as fortunate as I was, and a parent of a student will build one for you at his workbench. Thanks again, Mr. Mata!)

Divide the wheel into sections labeled with point values, "Free Spin," and "Lose Your Turn." Use the chalkboard or white board to show blanks that spell out a sentence or two from a current lesson. The team that states the mystery message exactly as it is written wins the game.

Examples:

_ _ _ _ _ _ _ _ , _ _ _ _ _ _ _ _ _ _ _ _ _ _ _ _ _ _ _
_ _ _ _ _ _ _ _ _ _ _ _ _ .

"Columbus's   flagship   was   called
the   Santa   Maria."

_ _
_ _ _ _ _ _ _ _ _ _ _ .

"Never   end   a   sentence   with   a
preposition."

The Dictionary Game

Player #1 chooses a word from the list below (or uses a different real word of his own choosing). She writes the word and its true definition on a card. On a separate card, she writes the word and a false definition, one that's meant to trick the other players. Each of the other players writes the word on a card along with a made-up definition.

The cards are collected by Player #1 who reads all the definitions aloud. Players guess which definition is correct. Points are awarded to 1) those who guess the correct definition and 2) those who have fooled players into choosing their false definitions. Player #2 starts the next round by selecting a different word, and play continues. Some words to consider for use in this game:

Syllabub: (noun) curdled cream served as a dessert.
Termagant: (noun) a scolding or nagging woman.
Stentorian: (adjective) extremely loud.
Commodious: (adjective) spacious or roomy.
Moodle: (verb) to dawdle aimlessly; to idle time away.
Crepuscular: (adjective) related to twilight, dim.
Verdant: (adjective) green or covered with green growth.
Raucous: (adjective) disorderly or unpleasant-sounding.
Blag: (verb) to rob or steal.
Imbroglio: (noun) a complicated argument.
Lachrymose: (adjective) causing weeping and tears.
Mucilaginous: (adjective) moist and sticky.
Polyglot: (noun) a person who knows several languages.
Beriberi: (noun) a disease causing pain and paralysis.
Parsimonious: (adjective) extremely frugal or stingy.
Bamboozle: (verb) to cheat by tricking or confusing.

The class should always be on the look-out for good words to use in The Dictionary Game.

Crossword Puzzles

The simplest way to create a crossword puzzle is
to select ten or twenty words, perhaps from a vocabulary
or spelling list, and place the words on graph paper or on a
computer-generated grid so the words intersect on
common letters, as shown.

    Start with the longest word on your list and write
it either across or down. Choose another word from the list
that shares a letter with the long word and write it by
intersecting it at the common letter. Continue in this
manner until all the words on the list are in place.

    Once all the words are situated, use the completed
puzzle as the answer sheet, and make a matching grid, leaving the spaces empty.
After that, there are two ways to proceed:

1) For older learners, clues are made for the answers going across and
   down, as in normal crossword puzzles found in newspapers and
   magazines. Thinking of good clues is often the part of puzzle-
   making that is the most fun. Good puzzle-makers pride themselves
   on creating playfully tricky clues. "Hawaiian hot stuff," for instance,
   is a clue for "lava." "Our 20th president's favorite comic strip" is
   "Garfield."

2) For younger learners, provide the list of words used in the puzzle.
   Challenge the players to complete the puzzle by counting the spaces
   in the grid and filling the spaces with words that fit.

There are many ways to use crossword puzzles in the classroom. Some
of the best puzzles are surprisingly simple, with just a handful of words, the
challenge coming mostly from the creatively-written clues.

As the leader of the games, you, the teacher, must be prepared to think
on your feet and be ready to change the rules to make the games fit the needs of
your class. Most of the time, you will be the one introducing the games, setting
them up, and directing play. Students, however, can eventually take more of a
role in preparing materials, giving directions, and being in charge of the games.

Letter Games

Action Alphabet

Write the letters of the alphabet on cards (put "Q" and "X" on one card). Students are arranged in a circle and each is given a card from the shuffled deck. Each student is to look at the letter on her card and write a verb beginning with that letter. When the teacher dings the bell, players pass their cards to the right. Each player receives a new card and writes a verb beginning with that letter, but cannot repeat a verb already written. If a player cannot think of a new verb by the time the bell is dinged (dung?), the card is passed on without a new word being written. Play continues until each player is holding his original card. Each player reads the list of verbs on his card, and the answers are discussed.

Variations: Instead of verbs, use nouns or adjectives. Make the game more competitive by having players drop out if they cannot think of a word before the bell dings. Play continues until just one person is left.

Match the Letter

The teacher prepares a worksheet with ten categories, such as: a sport, a street name in our town or neighborhood, a vegetable, a type of soup, a dessert, a breed of dog, something you'd see in the jungle, a famous singer, a TV show, a fruit. A letter is chosen. Let's say "B."

In one minute, each player fills in as many answers as he can: Baseball, Baxter Street, beet, borsht, banana split, bulldog, boa constrictor, etc. Each correct answer is worth three points. If more than one answer is filled in for a category (baseball, basketball), the player earns three points for the first answer and one point for each additional answer. The game can be played again and again, with a different letter each time.

Word Games

Word Building

The teacher (or leader) calls out three letters. Players are to make a list of words that contain the letters — in order. There may be other letters between. Examples:

w s e: waste, whisker, awesome...

s p l: splinter, simple, especially...

r s h: reshape, overshoe, marshmallow...

It's in the Cards

Split the class into four groups. Choose a long word that all the students know. Let's use "CONVERSATION" as an example. Make four identical decks of cards by writing "C" on four cards, "O" on four more cards, etc., until you have four decks, each containing the letters in "CONVERSATION." Shuffle the cards in each deck and give a deck to each group.

Challenge the players to arrange the letters to make words. One person in each group will write the group's words on a sheet of paper. (The players must play quietly; all the decks are the same, so if one group overhears another group's word, they will use the word themselves.) Words are accepted only if they can be spelled out with the cards — there is just one "C" and one "E" in "CONVERSATION," so the word "SCIENCE" cannot be used.

Three-letter words count for one point, four-letter words count for two, etc. Players should be told that, if put together correctly, all the letters in the deck will make one long word. Fifty points are awarded to any group able to put together the twelve-letter word. (Be warned: Kids will sometimes find naughty words when playing this game.)

Other possible words for use in this game: "QUARTERBACK," "PHOTOSYNTHESIS," "SATISFACTION," "TRANSPORTATION," "ELECTRICAL," "WATERMELON," "SATURDAY."

For extra fun, use a word that is an anagram for a term, such as "PUNISHMENT," the letters of which can be rearranged into "NINE THUMPS," or "DORMITORY," which can be reworked into "DIRTY ROOM."

Guess the Word

"I am thinking of a word with five letters. One of them is 'a.'"

"Is it 'paper'?"

"No, but another letter *is* 'p.'"

"Is it 'pants'?"

"No. Another letter is 's.'"

"Let's see. A. P. S. Is it 'traps'?"

"No, a fourth letter is 'e.'"

"A. P. S. E. Hmm. Is it 'paste'?"

"That's it! Now it's your turn to challenge us with a word."

Sentence Games

Vocabulary Hangman

To review the meanings of vocabulary words, or to sharpen sentence-writing skills, try this new twist on the old stand-by, Hangman. Divide the class into two teams. Think of a sentence that includes one of the vocabulary words. On the board, write the words of the sentence with blanks:

"$\underline{\ \ }\,\underline{\ \ }\,\underline{\ \ }\quad \underline{\ \ }\,\underline{\ \ }\,\underline{\ \ }\,\underline{\ \ }\,\underline{\ \ }\,\underline{\ \ }\,\underline{\ \ }\quad \underline{\ \ }\,\underline{\ \ }\,\underline{\ \ }\,\underline{\ \ }\quad \underline{\ \ }\,\underline{\ \ }\quad \underline{\ \ }\,\underline{\ \ }\,\underline{\ \ }\,\underline{\ \ }\,\underline{\ \ }\,\underline{\ \ }\,\underline{\ \ }\,\underline{\ \ }\quad \underline{\ \ }\,\underline{\ \ }\quad \underline{\ \ }\,\underline{\ \ }\,\underline{\ \ }\,\underline{\ \ }\,\underline{\ \ }\,\underline{\ \ }$"

("The **capital** city of Washington is Olympia.")

The teams take turn guessing letters. If a team chooses a letter that appears in the sentence, write the letter in the blank (or blanks) where it belongs and allow that team to continue with another guess. If a team chooses a letter that is not in the sentence, the team forfeits its turn and play continues with the other team making a guess. The game is won by the team that completes the sentence.

Put It Together

This game is much like Sentence Treasure Hunt on p. 53, but with Put It Together, we use a sentence (or an entire paragraph) from a real book, not one written by the teacher or the players themselves.

Divide the class into four or five groups. Select a sentence or a paragraph from a book and write the individual words on cards, making identical decks made up of the words in the sentence or paragraph. Give a deck of shuffled cards to each of the groups.

In ten minutes, which group comes closest to arranging the words just as they are in the book? Provide clues as needed: "The sentence begins with a noun." "The sentence ends with an eight-letter word." "This sentence came from a book by R. L. Stine."

1 + 2 + 3 Sentences

Divide the class into groups of four (extra players can be paired with partners to make the numbers work). Each player writes a noun on a piece of paper, folds the paper so the word cannot be seen, and passes the paper to the player sitting to the left. Each player now writes a verb on the paper, folds the paper again, and again passes it left. Each player now writes an adjective and passes the paper one more time.

Every player now holds a paper with a noun, a verb, and an adjective. The final task is to write a sentence using the three words. ("mother" + "dance" + "yellow" = "Her mother danced wearing yellow shoes.") Share the sentences and discuss. Challenge: Can your group write a story that includes *all four sentences*?

Chapter 8

Prepping for the World of Writing:
Critiques and Revision
Getting Published
Rejections: A Part of the Process
Creativity's Quirks and Pitfalls

The life of a writer has its highs and lows. While we hope the highs are many (with some being *really* high) and the lows are few (and nothing too extreme), we acknowledge that everything worth doing in life carries some risk.

In this chapter, we take a look at some of the things that tend to intimidate a hard-working writer. Fear and worry always insist on tagging along with creative people on the road to success, but they don't have to be accepted as traveling companions. They can be told, firmly and decisively, to *buzz off.*

Critiques and Revision

Critiques

Consider how your duties as a writing teacher differ from those of your colleagues. When a math teacher collects her students' papers, she hopes each paper is exactly the same, with all the answers correct to the last detail. For a creative writing teacher, the assignments will not — cannot — all read the same.

Your greatest pleasure is in finding creative phrasings, unexpected plot twists, and other elements of good writing that impel you to take a red pen and indicate approval with a star, a smiley face, or the word "Excellent!" Reading new stories and poems is the best part of being a writing teacher. And when you find a real gem, I hope you jump at the chance to read it aloud to the class. That's another thing math teachers do not do.

As a teacher of writing, you will be required to critique your students' work. You will read their stories and make useful and encouraging comments and suggestions. You will also teach your students how to critique each other's work…and their own.

> *Real writers enjoy having their work*
> *critiqued. They look forward to it,*
> *almost crave it. They welcome suggestions*
> *and corrections, because they know*
> *their stories aren't perfect, and that mistakes*
> *are often invisible to the people who*
> *make them. Most real writers belong to a*
> *critique group, a small number of like-*
> *minded and similarly-skilled individuals*
> *with whom they meet regularly and share*
> *their work. Writers who want their*
> *writing taken seriously ought to find*
> *a critique group to join, and if*
> *there isn't one, they ought to start one.*

Ten Critiquing Guidelines

1. A 'critique' is a detailed opinion or review of a piece of writing. The word "critique" is related to the word "criticize," which, for some people, implies disapproval, but your students should know that the real definition of "criticize" is "to make judgments," and judgments don't always have to be negative. Movie critics often rave about a new film, saying it's the best of the year and is sure to win many Academy Awards. The critic made a critique and criticized the movie without saying anything negative. So, when it is time to critique each other's stories in class, it doesn't mean that it's time to point out all the things that are wrong with the stories.

2. Require all writing assignments to be double-spaced and with wide margins all around. The person doing the critique will then have room to

use a pen of contrasting color to write between the lines and in the margins.

3. Every writer must expect — and accept — compliments and suggestions, essential parts of the writing process.

4. When critiquers (yes, the word "critiquer," defined as "one who critiques," is in some modern dictionaries) find fault, they must strive to state things in a positive way. That means they try to avoid the words "no" and "not" wherever possible. It feels better to hear "Walk" than "Do not run," and, in critiquing a story, "Try 'ridiculous' here" is better than "Don't use 'silly' again." Changing a single word can sometimes help to express a thought more positively. "The school stays open until 5 o'clock" sounds better than "The school closes at 5 o'clock." When writing a critique, try "This sentence needs work," not "This sentence is no good." Some news needs to be broken gently.

5. Critiquers must be able to spot good sentences, good word choice, and good plot development. If you knew a carpenter who had just built a house, could you walk around and point out some of his good work? Of course. Could you find something you would have done differently? Most likely, but a friend would accentuate the positive. Think of it this way: Could you take five different pizzas from five different restaurants and list things you like about each, as well as what you don't like so much? We can find good and bad in everything. Judgments are sure to be made when a critiquer examines a writing assignment. When I critique a piece of writing I try to point out three good things for every part I find not so good. And I don't draw attention to every fault I notice, because what I *don't* want is for my fellow writer to become discouraged or overwhelmed. Improvement is our goal, not perfection, and improvement always comes a little at a time, not all at once.

6. When doing a critique, try to see the whole piece, not the individual parts. A writer wants her critiquer to see the *story*, not the separate words or individual sentences. The first thing the writer wants to know is if you liked the story, if you understood the meaning. She doesn't

want to hear about a spelling mistake, or a clumsily-written sentence, or some other small piece of the whole. It is important to see the entire piece, to determine its purpose, and to respond to what the writer is trying to say. We don't view an art piece square inch by square inch, giving our opinion of the small piece in the upper left corner. We respond to the whole picture, then comment, perhaps, on the colors used for the sky, or the expression on Mona Lisa's face.

7. When doing critiques in class, sometimes it is best to focus on a single element. "Remember yesterday, when we talked about using the five senses in our writing? Let's go over today's paper and find places where we did this well and where we could do better. This will give you the opportunity to change 'He was scared,' for instance, to 'He hid in the musty closet, frozen, listening to the short pulls of his own breath...'"

8. The writing teacher must be careful not to critique in such a way that students feel they need to write to please the teacher. Middle school students sometimes write with a bit of an edge or with questionable language or attitude. Any such issues must be addressed without quashing creativity. One rule of thumb is to say, "I notice that you..." instead of "I like that you..." or "I don't like that you..."

9. When stories are being read aloud in class, all students must listen and be respectful if offering comments. "When you used the word 'grungy,' it really made me feel what you were feeling." "You're good at reading your stories aloud with so much emotion." Negative criticisms are to be phrased as kindly as possible. No: "That story was completely confusing, and I didn't know what you were talking about." Yes: "Your sentences were a little too long for me. I think you would make yourself clearer if you shortened them a little." Student critiquers can offer two compliments for every fault. And they should be reminded that there is no good reason to withhold or to be stingy with compliments.

10. We writers are not drawing from a limited supply, like a group of people sharing a pizza, where if one person has more, others have less. We writers can *all* have more. In the classroom, if one student's story is well

done, it doesn't mean the next one must balance things out by being boring and tedious. I have been in classrooms and critique groups where every participant at a given time produced excellent work, and all contributors left feeling good about what each had accomplished. Twenty people sharing stories can discover that *all* the stories are good.

As your students become adept at doing critiques for others, they will get better at self-editing their own work. As they write, they will anticipate what a classmate might say in a critique, so they try a little harder to write it better in the first place.

Try This:

Critiquing Real Authors

Choose a passage from a published book and analyze it together. Assign some of the students to be complimentary and others to be negatively critical. "Is this an example of good writing? Can you see and feel what is happening in the scene? Could the author have chosen better words? If you like a sentence, what makes it so good? If you're confused by something, what makes it confusing?"

Revision

Even big-name authors don't write their best stuff on the first try. With the help of editors, they go over their stories again and again until everything is as perfect as they can possibly get it. To be good writers, your students must accept the fact that revision is necessary. It is a part of the world of a writer.

I have had students dash off stories, expecting immediate approval. And 100% of the time they got it: "I like the way you started this story with such a bang." "The verbs you used make your story come alive." But they also — every time — were told to revise. That's when I would hear, "I'm not writing it all over again!" As if they had just climbed Mt. Everest and I had told them to go back down and climb it again.

I did not expect them to scrap the whole story and start from scratch. Much of what they had written was good just as it was and needed to be kept. But every story I've ever seen has needed some cleaning up or retooling.

"Compare your story to a car," I'd tell my students. "I like your car. It's very nice. It doesn't belong in a junk yard, but I do want you to fix it so the engine hums, then polish the whole thing until it sparkles and shines. In other words, I want you to take something that is already pretty good and make it even better."

> *"Revise" does not mean "rewrite."*

A concert pianist practices long and hard, correcting her mistakes, improving her finger work. When she first attempts to play a Mozart sonata, she doesn't play it just once and say "That's it. I played it once and I'm not playing it anymore." If she wants to be a great pianist, she must work through the rough spots, then bring it all up to speed. She makes that sonata "sparkle and shine."

Too many young writers — especially those who are reluctant to write in the first place — whip off a story and think they are finished. "I'm done!" they announce, sliding the paper across the desk. They have yet to learn that after writing a first draft, *they are not done.* When a student declares "I'm done!" he should be told that he isn't even "done" with that sentence. "You mean you're done *for now.*"

Compare the writing process to getting dressed in the morning. Saying "I'm done" after finishing the first draft of a writing assignment is about as silly as saying "I'm done" after putting on one article of clothing. No, you are not done. There are many steps in the process and you have finished one of them. Real writers understand the importance of revision and make it a part of their practice. In fact, real authors often look at their books *after they've been published* and wish they could still make changes.

Stephen King, in *The Bazaar of Bad Dreams*, wrote: "Until a writer either retires or dies, the work is not finished; it can always use another polish and a few more revisions." Never satisfied, Walt Whitman endlessly revised *Leaves of Grass*. He died at the age of 72 and received the ninth and final edition on his deathbed.

96

A Note About Grammar:

Nobody is perfect. Even great writers make mistakes with the language (in writing or speaking — good writers are expected to do both well). Grammar is important in the writing classroom, but it should be worked on "as you go." When we stop to make corrections in grammar and spelling, the writing suffers. On a trip, we don't stop every half mile to check the air in the tires and refill the car with gas. When writing, we get into the flow without fear of being corrected during the flow. We review the grammar and spelling after the story is finished. Each batter on a baseball team has a different style when swinging the bat. If the coach wants to correct a player's swing, he does it at practice, not during the game. Though not perfect, a player's swing may still be effective. Players with "incorrect" swings, in spite of their problems, sometimes hit the ball over the centerfield fence.

Four Revision Tips

A serious writer learns to rely on favorite books and websites when questions concerning grammar and language arise. An ever-growing familiarity with the rules of writing is essential. The following tips will be especially helpful to beginning writers:

1. **Learn to CUT.** When revising a first draft, a writer might attempt to clarify blurry plot twists and confusing character motivations by adding better details, which can be a sensible strategy. Doing just the opposite — taking words away — is another good plan of attack. Mark Twain once apologized in a letter to a friend: "Sorry for writing such a long letter; I  didn't have time to write a short one." Sometimes we have to be like butchers cutting fat from the meat. Cultivating the skill of cutting unnecessary words from a story is one of the most satisfying tasks in the life of a writer, but it isn't always easy. Well-written sentences, paragraphs, even whole chapters might have to go.

2. **Know what to cut.** Like a gardener knowing which are the vegetables and which are the weeds, a writer must know which words to keep and which to cut. Do a search on the computer to check for overused words. In a story about a giant, "big" might have to be replaced with synonyms. Search for "there is" and "there are," both of which are often overused. ("Two dogs barked" is better than "There were two dogs barking.") To help your story's flow, be a surgeon and take a scalpel to the word "that" when it isn't really needed. ("He said ~~that~~ I was his best friend.")

3. **Avoid cramming information into a small space.** In trying to cut and condense, the unskilled writer will sometimes force a lot of information into a tight space. "John, on his way to visit his friend Paul, the goalie on the hockey team, kept thinking about what he had said during math class today to Katie, the girl he wanted to ask to the dance on Saturday." What a mess. In one sentence, we have information about three different characters; good luck to the reader trying to disentangle it. No real writer ever said writing is easy. Anything difficult — climbing a mountain, playing *Embryonic Journey* on the guitar, doing a fancy trick on a skateboard — takes time and great effort, but the reward is there at the end.

4. **Know when to stop.** Just as a writer shouldn't overload his readers with too much information at the beginning of a story, he shouldn't explain every little detail at the end. Allow the readers to put two and two together for themselves. If a story involves a main character in a spot of trouble, it can end shortly after the trouble is resolved.

The Revision Checklist

When the first draft of a writing assignment is finished, allow the students to use a checklist, like the one below, to score themselves before submitting the work to you. If desired, individuals may ask a classmate to use the checklist to offer scores as well. The writers will then have some good ideas for how to proceed with revision. The areas of focus can be changed with each assignment. Note: The heading labeled "Self" is here twice because each writer should revise her work *at least* twice before submitting it.

	Self	Teacher/Peer	Self
Structure			
Clever Start			
Good Details			
Well-chosen Words			
Clear and Consistent			
Snappy Ending			
Spelling			

Notes:

"Structure": What is the overall look, including layout, margins, indented paragraphs, and neatness?

"Clever start": Is there a good opening sentence that draws the reader into the story?

99

"Good Details": Are there plenty of good details? Did you show whole scenes?

"Well-chosen Words": How vivid is the language? Did you exercise your vocabulary? Are there any key words repeated too often?

"Clear and Consistent": Is there confusion with plot or characters? Do the readers have a good idea of what you set out to tell them?

"Snappy Ending": Does the ending tie together the elements presented in the beginning? Does the ending leave the reader feeling satisfied?

"Spelling": Did you keep the spelling mistakes to a reasonable number? Are there two or three corrections that would make the story more fluid and enjoyable?

> *When critiquing, overlook spelling mistakes that don't affect the meanings of sentences. For instance, when a writer mistypes the word "the" as "teh," we realize what has happened and read around the mistake. Sometimes, though, we must use that red pen of ours. Misspelling "friend" as "fiend" has led to some peculiar story twists. And the writer of this sentence meant to say "violin": "Einstein started taking villain lessons when he was six."*

Editing Practice — Science Biographies

It is good for young writers to know that **all writers make plenty of mistakes**. And some can be rather amusing.

Very young students focus on the writing of the individual letters as they work so hard to complete a single sentence. Older children produce sentences at a much faster clip, and will need different types of editing help as they continue to improve, trying new forms and styles of writing.

My middle school science students had become quite inventive in their approaches, as was evident when they wrote mini-biographies of famous scientists. Most of the students were moderately well-read and increasingly intrigued with the techniques used by their favorite authors. In emulating them, the students sometimes overreached and needed editing help, the likes of which they hadn't needed when they were younger and less experimental. Examples:

1. **The "I-can't-argue-with-that" introduction:** "When Galileo was born, no one guessed that the drooling little baby would someday be a world-famous scientist." While I'm sure that is true, I am *not* sure it's such a good way to start a biography. It was a popular way, however, among my students. One writer even got us inside the head of the little baby: "Not thinking he would become the most important scientist of the 20th century, Albert Einstein was born on March 14th, 1879, in Ulm, Germany." Authors, indeed, have some amazing abilities, but *come on*.

2. **The folksy introduction:** "Many of you have heard of Isaac Newton, but if you think you already know everything about him, guess again and keep on reading, because I have a story to tell."

3. **Inserting personal prejudices:** Perhaps this student should have done a little more research on the life of Newton to see what other factors kept him from hearing wedding bells: "Isaac Newton must have been ugly or something because he never got married." Poor Newton takes his lumps again, from this writer who couldn't hide his disappointment in the non-exciting manner of Newton's death. "When Isaac Newton was 84 years old, he died only of old age."

4. **The information rush:** Perhaps this writer had been working very hard, it was getting late, and she wanted to be finished with the assignment, so she rushed through a number of long, eventful years and squished them all into a sentence or two. Gotta get to sleep, you know! "Albert Einstein married his wife Mileva and she became pregnant with a baby girl named Lieserl. They had some trouble, so they got a divorce, and he later married his cousin, Elsa Einstein Lowenthal."

5. **The brown-noser:** "So, as you read, you can see that Newton had a busy life. Hopefully, we can follow his example by showing interest in school and trying our best to get good grades."

6. **The simplified conclusion:** "Thanks to Jacques Charles, we now know not to leave inflated balloons inside hot cars on summer days."

7. **At death do we part:** "Unfortunately, all good things eventually come to an end, and Mendeleev died in 1907 from being very, very ill." "…but like everyone else in the world, Einstein could not live forever, and he died on April 18, 1955 in Princeton, New Jersey."

> *Periods, commas, and other punctuation marks might seem small and insignificant, but consider the difference between these two statements: "Mommy, I can always tell when you've been to the beauty shop by the way you smell." "Mommy, I can always tell when you've been to the beauty shop. By the way, you smell."*

Getting Published

For students involved in the *We Think With Ink* program, "getting published" simply means that a story or poem is printed in a place where many people can see it and react to it. The most likely way for this to happen is through the making of a class booklet of stories. Booklets are made once a month, showcasing work produced in class. The booklets are distributed to families, to the school library, and other appropriate outlets.

Opinion pieces can be submitted to the local newspaper's editorial page. Stories can be entered in contests conducted by companies and organizations. And, for those striving for the gold, there are magazine publishers, such as *Skipping Stones* and *Stone Soup*, that accept submissions from children.

Letters to the Editor

A good way for beginning writers to see their work published is through the editorial page of the local newspaper. (Small-town newspapers are more likely to accept student letters of opinion than those of big cities, but never say never.) Children have strong opinions and, if expressed well, others in the community will be interested. When I was a third-grade teacher, every year a few of my students' letters were chosen for publication. For a week or so, those kids walked with an extra spring in their step, happy for the attention they received.

Items in the news often spur a young writer to express an opinion. Child-related news items — the removal of a favorite playground, funding for the local swimming pool, etc. — are ideal. Issues concerning the environment or the treatment of animals strike a chord with kids. One of my third-grade students had a letter published in which he begged the city to refrain from tearing down his favorite restaurant as part of a plan to widen the highway.

Teachers, keep your eyes open for news items that will spur students into writing letters for the editorial page. Feed them the facts, and encourage them to write. You may assist in the editing of such letters, but do not clean them up to the point where the students' voices are lost.

Students may feel that a story they have written is worthy of being published in a national magazine or even by one of the established book publishers. **It is not easy for anyone to get published by a major publishing house.** That's the bad news. Here's the good:

When a hospital hires a doctor, they don't consider anyone who hasn't been thoroughly trained at a medical school. When a school system needs a new teacher, they demand to see a diploma and a license. No one even thinks of applying for a job as a lawyer, or an electrical engineer, or a microbiologist without credentials from an accredited college or university.

But when a publishing company wants to put out a new book, the editors go through the manuscripts that have been submitted through the postal service or e-mail. If there is a story they like, they don't ask if the author is a college graduate or if she has a degree. They are looking for someone who has written a good book.

That is why regular people — butchers, bakers, candlestick makers — who have creative imaginations and a natural flair for writing, sometimes make the bestseller list. (Don't misunderstand: Getting published is not easy. In most cases, those who find success have worked hard at it, attending countless seminars and workshops, writing and submitting and being rejected many, many times. But published writers often do not have a degree from a university.)

So, yes, teachers, in their spare time, have had books published. Forest rangers, yoga instructors, and garbage collectors, too. And students have had success in getting stories accepted by big publishers.

For those curious about what it takes to get a story published by a major book publisher, here is a rough idea of the process:

1. You write a story.

2. You go over it, fixing the problems and mistakes, taking out unnecessary words and parts, making everything clear, as perfect as can be.

3. You put the story away for a while. A few days. Two weeks. Enough time so you'll be able to look at it with fresh eyes.

4. You fix it some more, trying to make it perfect, all the while knowing that it's impossible to make it really, *really* perfect.

5. You show it to someone. A friend. A writing partner. A teacher. The members of your critique group. You listen to what others have to say. You consider their suggestions, especially if several people have the same opinion, but **you don't have to make every change they suggest**.

104

6. You work at it and work at it. Then you work at it some more. If you find yourself struggling and unsure of how to proceed, consider writing the story from a different point of view or switching from third-person to first-person. Then repeat steps 3 and 4.

7. You show the story to someone again. Consider any ideas for improvement.

8. When you think your story is as good as it can possibly be, you prepare to send it to a publisher. To do this, you go on-line, or refer to the *Writer's Market* or another respected publication. Search for a publisher that is looking for the kind of story you have written.

9. After finding a suitable publisher, you write a cover letter to go with your story. This should be a one-page letter that tells something about yourself and the story you have written. The *Writer's Market*, as well as sources on-line, will have suggestions for how to write a good cover letter.

10. You submit the story, and you wait for a reply.

Sometimes it takes six months or longer to hear from a publisher, and usually in the end the answer is no. Again, getting published is not easy. What keeps a writer motivated is the opportunity to get a "yes" someday. Go to the library and look at all the books on the shelves. Each one of those books represents someone somewhere who got "yes" for an answer.

So, your story is finished, you made it ready for delivery, you've sent it in. Now what? Now you try to forget about it. You get busy with new stories. If the story you submitted is indeed rejected, you send it to a different publisher, *and you keep looking forward.*

Rejections: A Part of the Process

The word "rejection" has an unkind ring to it, but that is the word we use when a publisher decides not to buy a story being offered. Rejection is a big part of the world of a writer. When you send a story to a publisher, you are presenting an invitation, and invitations are often rejected, for any number of reasons.

"Would you like a cookie?"

"No, thank you."

Is the cookie being rejected because it is bad? *What's wrong with the cookies I made? Why doesn't he want one? Oh, no! Something's wrong with me!* Wait a minute. Just think of all the reasons for why a person might say "no" to a cookie. Maybe he just had a cookie (or ten). Maybe he has an allergy and sees nuts in the cookie. Maybe it's almost time for supper. Maybe he has a stomach ache, or a toothache. Maybe he just *doesn't want* a cookie right now.

When a story of yours gets rejected, **do not assume that the story isn't good or that you are not a good writer.** Publishing companies get hundreds of submissions every week. The editors don't have time to give detailed reasons for why they don't want your story. There are many possible reasons for a rejection, so why not assume that the publisher liked your story, but just couldn't use it at this time. That's fine. Now send it to someone else. **Keep trying.**

We writers send stories to publishers the way we cast lines into the water when fishing. We're surprised if a fish bites right away. We're happy if we catch one or two fish after a whole afternoon in the boat. Even if the fish never bite, we enjoy the day anyway, out in the fresh air on the quiet lake, taking in the clouds, the trees, the loons…the smells, the sounds, *the experience.* When it comes right down to it, it doesn't really matter if the fish ever bite.

It's the same with your stories. The writing of the story is the reward, the way you feel inside as the characters come alive and the plot takes shape. Sure, it's exciting to think that an editor might like the story enough to accept it for publication, but if she chooses to pass on the opportunity, that's okay too. Would you get mad or feel ashamed if you cast a line into the water and none of the fish chose to nibble? Of course not.

For me as a writer, if an editor "bites" at my offer of a story, good. If he doesn't, that's fine as well. I will still go on writing. Nothing will stop me. **If a psychic with a crystal ball looked into the future and told me that nothing I write will ever get published,** *I would still write.* I enjoy it that much. It does that much for me. I know in my heart, however, that if I keep on trying, I almost certainly will get published, just as if you keep fishing on that lake, you almost certainly will catch a fish sooner or later.

Every published writer has tales to tell of being rejected over and over before finally getting a "yes." The writers who never succeed are the ones who fail to try. True, if you never send anything in, you'll be spared the "anguish" of being rejected, but you'll never experience the thrill of being accepted either.

Don't be afraid of rejection. When you send stories to publishers, of course the answer will be "no" almost every time. That's the way it is. You aren't supposed to get a "yes" most of the time. Consider this: If you caught a fish every time you put your hook in the water, you'd quickly lose interest in the challenge of fishing. (You'd even get rather irritated, because fishing is supposed to be relaxing, and how relaxing can it be if you have to keep removing hooks from the mouths of fish every minute?)

Many people consider Henry Aaron the best home run hitter of all time. He hit one every 16 times he came to the plate. That means that for every 16 times he tried, 15 times he *failed* to hit a home run. When he didn't hit one, he didn't pout, or feel ashamed, or quit. Henry Aaron expected to fail most of the time, just as we writers must expect our work to not get published most of the time. Being rejected makes the successes — when they come — so much sweeter.

Think of it this way: Playing darts is fun even if you don't get a bullseye on every throw. We're surprised when we do occasionally hit the little circle in the middle of the target. In the same way, we writers send in our stories or poems, not expecting to get good news every time, or even much of the time.

Everyone from Beatrix Potter to J. K. Rowling has been rejected. When it happens to us, we need to be persistent, not bothered or discouraged. The difference between a writer who is published and one who is not is that one did not give up and the other one did. **Persistence works.**

107

Always keep in mind that a rejection is just one person's opinion, and often that person is *just plain wrong.* Consider these famous misjudgments:

"This 'telephone' has too many shortcomings to be seriously considered as a means of communication. The device is of no value to us." — Western Union internal memo, 1876.

"Who…wants to hear actors talk?" — H. M. Warner (Warner Brothers), 1927.

"We don't like their sound, and guitar music is on the way out." — Decca Recording Co. rejecting the Beatles, 1962.

"There is no reason anyone would want a computer in their home." — Ken Olson, president, chairman, and founder of Digital Equipment Corp., 1977.

"Everything that can be invented has been invented." — Charles H. Duell, Commissioner, U.S. Office of Patents, 1899.

One more thing: Dr. Seuss's first book, *And to Think That I Saw It on Mulberry Street,* was rejected by 27 publishers before finding a home at Random House. One of the rejection letters said Seuss's writing was "too different" from the other books for children on the market. Obviously, his millions of readers liked his quirky — "different" — style. Thank goodness Dr. Seuss didn't give up on himself.

Creativity's Quirks and Pitfalls

In a room full of creative people (your classroom, perhaps?), egos can clash. Some of the greatest rock bands, made up of highly creative individuals, were undone by egos scraping and colliding. As the teacher, you must be prepared to deal with such matters as you encourage creative thinking in the classroom.

A common problem arises when one writer accuses another of "stealing" an idea. The simplest way to deal with this problem is to stress **the importance of writers keeping their ideas to themselves as they write.**

We Think With Ink

There are two dangers in talking about a story before writing it. First, when a writer *tells* others about his quirky characters and cool plot twists, much of the desire to do the hard work of writing disappears. If everyone already knows what's going to happen in the story, why bother writing it? The other hazard in talking too much and writing too little is that someone else can take the ideas and run with them. Writers need to learn how to clam up.

That said, your students need to understand that coincidences occur. A writer can have a terrific idea for a story, only to find that someone else had the *very same idea.* That happens, in the classroom and in the world of publishing.

It's horribly discouraging to submit a well-written story with a terrific plot and then find out that last year someone in a distant state had the very same idea, and that person's book is currently in production. If such a thing happens, the writer's only recourse is to get back on the horse and write something new.

Try This:

"Think Alone/Think Alike"

For this game, give each student in the class a 3x5 card or a piece of paper of about that size.

"Put your name at the top and number the paper 1, 2, 3. I'll ask three questions. You write the answers. Don't worry about spelling; if I can read what you're trying to say, it will count. Whoever has the most correct answers at the end, wins the game.

"As the leader of the game, I am the judge. I promise to be as open-minded as possible, but I might have to tell you that your answer is not acceptable, and my word is final.

"Ready? Number 1: Write the name of a president of the United States." (Allow time for students to write their answers.) "Number 2: Write the name of a fruit." Again, allow time for writing. "Number 3: Write the name of a holiday."

When the students are finished, collect the papers. Hold the papers in your hand and say, "Oh, I forgot to tell you. You don't get a point for an answer if someone else had the same answer as you." Now go through the papers, commenting on the answers as you sort them into piles.

109

We Think With Ink

"The first one says 'Lincoln.' Good answer. The next one says 'Washington.' Very good. Uh-oh. This next one says 'Washington,' so both of these go into the discard pile. Oops, here's another 'Lincoln.' Too bad…"

Most of the time the answers are limited to the current president, Washington, and Lincoln, so the discard pile will be very large. A few students — those who think differently — will have John Quincy Adams, Rutherford B. Hayes, or some other president. They get points.

If someone writes "Benjamin Franklin" or "Martin Luther King," be sure to point out that the first requirement is to provide a correct answer. The second requirement is to be only one to have that answer. Since neither Franklin nor King ever served as president, those answers must go into the discard pile.

Often at the end of the scoring for the first question, just two or three players have a point. Gather the papers back into a pile and proceed to the fruit answers. You'll most likely see a lot of apples, oranges, and bananas. For the third question, the popular answers are Christmas and the Fourth of July.

The winner of this little game will perhaps have a score of one or two. Many will be stuck at zero, unhappy and complaining. This is a good time to tell the class that this was just a practice round and that you'll now play the game again, with all the rules in place.

"There will be five questions this time, so number your paper 1, 2, 3, 4, 5." ("Think Alone/Think Alike" can be played with any number of questions. With scoring and discussion, a game of five questions played with a class of twenty or thirty students will take about a half an hour. If you have more time, for an even more interesting game, try eight or ten questions.)

Proceed with the game by reading these directions to get five responses from each player:

1. Name something that is usually yellow and not any other color. ("Shirt" is not a good answer, since shirts can be any color. Even though some bananas are green, most bananas we see are yellow, so "bananas" is accepted. With all the many answers to choose from — mustard, lemons, the middle traffic light, the sun, a dandelion, a taxi cab, a canary, a brick on the road to Oz — don't accept lazy answers like "yellow paint" or "a yellow crayon.")
2. A farm animal.
3. A city in our state that starts with M or S.
4. Something you eat that starts with R.

110

5. Someone in this room. (This one involves more luck than the others, but part of the lesson is that creativity sometimes involves luck.)

After the answers are written, collect the papers. Assign a couple of the students to tally scores at the board. Then read the answers aloud as you sort the papers. "Something yellow: The sun. Egg yolks. My grandpa's teeth. A banana. A goldfinch. The sun. Oops, the two slips that say 'sun' go in the discard pile. Lemon meringue pie. A light bulb that's turned on. A Green Bay Packer's football helmet. A bee. A school bus. A banana. Uh-oh, 'banana' was used. The sun. That's another discard..." Continue until all the slips have been read. Those in the pile that survive the winnowing are named, and tallies are made on the board. Then the slips are gathered up and the responses for #2 are read.

Be sure to make a fuss when an especially creative response is given. "A cucumber left in the garden too long" will turn yellow, so that's a good answer and almost sure to be unmatched. I also approve of players earning points for being specific — "lemon" will earn a point, and so will "lemon meringue pie," as will "lemon Jell-o." Remind the players that if something creative doesn't come to mind, they should write down the obvious. Sometimes two players cancel each other with "lemon meringue pie" and no one says just "lemon."

Why We Play "Think Alone/Think Alike"

Although a writer thinks creatively, somebody else in the world — maybe even someone in the same room — might be thinking the same way. This means that sometimes a very good idea doesn't get the attention it deserves, a cruel fact for which young writers must be prepared.

"Think Alone/Think Alike" should be played frequently throughout the school year. It will help students accept the fact that there are pitfalls in the road to being creative. It also keeps minds sharp and always on the lookout for unique ideas, turns of phrase, and really good words.

Yes, even individual words in a story must pass the "Think Alone/Think Alike" test. Imagine a group of writers working on a story that takes place on a summer afternoon in the Mojave Desert. Twenty of them describe the conditions by writing, "It was very hot." Three writers use the phrase "The sun was burning hot." One writes: "The blistering sun blazed in the sky." Another tells it like this: "The sun sizzled everything that moved." Those last two will make readers — perhaps even an editor at a publishing house — sit up and take notice. There

111

is always the chance of two writers using the same phrase in exactly the same way, but such an occurrence is unlikely when truly creative writing takes place.

> *Getting published usually involves some luck.*

One more good thing about "Think Alone/Think Alike": During the game, no one cheats by peeking at other people's responses. If a player were to accidentally see what his neighbor wrote, he'd be foolish to write it on his own paper. The answers would cancel each other out, and he wouldn't earn any points.

More Topics for "Think Alone/Think Alike":

Name a famous American in history, or a famous singer, or athlete, or...
Name a player on the Packers, or Yankees, or Lakers...
Name a president after Lincoln...
Name a musical instrument, a vegetable, a candy bar...
Name a street in our town...
Name a word with three different vowels...
Name something you might see at a fair, at the beach, in the sky...
Name the title of a book by Dr. Seuss, of a Disney movie, or...
Name a city in the world that starts with C or J or W or...
Name a country that starts with T or L or S or...
Name something that is usually red or green or blue or...
Name something you can eat that starts with N or P or D or...

Add your own ideas to the list. Be creative. The sky's the limit.

Chapter 9

Some Final Tips for Teachers, Students, and Writers

Twenty Ways to Improve Your Writing and to Increase Your Chances of Being Published

1. **Know the rules of good writing.** Incorrect language is all around you every day. It's on TV, in the music you listen to, in the slang-filled conversations you have with your friends. **If you hear incorrect language often enough, it begins to *sound* correct.** Writers need to be mindful of the rules of grammar and the elements of story structure. To keep you on your game, read and reread language- and grammar-related books and websites — there are so many good ones. Note: As much as we want to follow the rules of writing, we don't have to be overly rigid. Incomplete sentences, for example, are allowable. Even preferable. See?

> *"Good English, well-spoken and well-written, will open more doors than a college degree. Bad English will slam doors you didn't even know existed."*
> *— William Raspberry*

2. **Write a lot.** "Unless I write every day," Charlie Chaplin once said, "I don't feel I deserve my dinner." The best way to become a good writer is to *write*.

3. **Read a lot.** Read for enjoyment, but as you're reading, notice what the author is doing. Following the example of other writers is an excellent way to develop your writing skills. As a writer, you must watch for and

113

recognize strong sentences, authentic dialog, even **single words** that provide great punch. We writers have to teach ourselves how to listen and to notice. Why do you reread certain sentences or paragraphs in books? For the same reason that that one particular line in your favorite movie always puts a lump in your throat. The words were put together *just right.*

4. **Write down the story ideas that come to mind.** If you don't, you'll probably forget them. This is especially true for ideas that come to you when you're in bed half asleep. You think you'll remember, but you won't. Keep a notebook at your bedside and write down the ideas. All writers know that while some "tremendous" ideas that come in the night turn out to be complete nonsense in the light of day, occasional nuggets of gold are there waiting in the morning.

5. **When editing your work, be careful of what you're throwing away or deleting.** Well-written sentences, as well as entire early story drafts, should be stored in a file for later. Immersed in the writing of a new story, you could find the perfect spot for a piece of a story written long ago, tucked away in a scrap file.

6. **Be able to summarize your story in one sentence.** When someone asks you, "What's your story about?" she doesn't want a long rambling account. She wants a short, straightforward sentence or two. To get an idea of how to skillfully summarize, read what's written on the jacket flaps or on the backs of books.

7. **Write about what you know.** I would have a hard time writing a story about a woman grinding corn meal in a village in Zambia. That isn't who I am. I wouldn't know what that woman is thinking, what might have happened to her yesterday, what she is looking forward to doing tomorrow. Someone else will have to tell her story, someone who has lived in — or who has at least once visited — her village. We are at our best when we are writing about the things we know, which is good, because every one of us knows a lot about many different things, and what we know is of interest to others.

8. **Show, don't tell.** Instead of writing "He was furious," *show* with words that he was furious. Remember the power of verbs. Have the character kick something, shake something, *do* something. Let your readers figure it out for themselves. Without you *telling* them, make your readers say, "Wow, was that guy ever mad!"

9. **Keep your point of view consistent.** If we're experiencing a story from the point of view of Character A, we see and hear and feel everything Character A sees and hears and feels, and we are allowed to know what Character A is thinking and planning. We are not, however, allowed inside the heads of Characters B or C. We cannot know what they are thinking and feeling and plotting, because we are not experiencing the story from their points of view. On a similar note: If a story begins in first person ("I" and "me"), it cannot change to third person ("he" and "him").

10. **Avoid clichés.** "As mad as a wet hen" is a cliché. Think of something fresh ("as mad as a wasp with a headache") or stay away from similes altogether. As suggested earlier, *show* that a character is mad by having him *do* something: kicking a chair across the room, pulling his own hair until it hurts, yelling bloody murder—oops, that's a cliché.

11. **Be specific.** Say "chickadee," not "bird." Say "cottonwood," not "tree."

12. **Use surprising and unpredictable details.** The best writers know how to use vivid and concrete details to draw the reader *into* the story, to make the reader see, hear, smell, feel, even taste what is going on in the lives of the characters. Compare these two sentences: "He remembered that mean man yelling at him in the mall." "A shiver rippled down his spine as he recalled the man with the yellow teeth and the splotchy face ripping into him in front of the Bullseye Arcade." Your stories are only as good as the details you put into them.

115

13. **Don't include dull information.** "Wesley got up from the couch. He scratched an itch on his elbow as he looked out the window. They had said on TV that the rain was supposed to stop, but the drizzle continued. Wesley coughed. He thought about making a sandwich, but he really wasn't very hungry, so he decided to wait until lunch time. His phone rang..." That information might be realistic, but it isn't interesting. Boil it down to: "Wesley got up from the couch and looked out at the rain. His phone rang..." Alfred Hitchcock said a good story is "life, with the dull parts taken out." Hurry up and get to the good stuff.

14. **Use all five senses.** In doing so, you bring the reader right into the action. In our day-to-day lives, most of us rely heavily on our sense of sight. However, when we think back to the best times of our lives, much of what we remember with great clarity involves sounds, touches, smells, and tastes, so we can't ignore those senses in our writing. **Try this:** Get a set of five highlighters, each of a different color. Go through one of your stories and highlight all the sensory details, using a different color for each sense: sight, sound, taste, smell, and touch. You'll see at a glance which senses you favor and which you neglect. The numbers don't have to be equal, but if there is a scene in which a character enters a room and sees flowers on the table, a clock on the mantel, a portrait of a woman on the wall, and a man lighting a candle, you may want to balance things out a bit. The character can smell the cinnamon-scented candle and hear the ticking of the clock. By adding sensory details, you will enrich your story and allow your readers to experience the scene as if they were there.

15. **Consider the "Power of Three."** In some stories, on the third try the main character finally succeeds. Children's stories often follow this formula.

16. **Cut unneeded words.** If you use good nouns and verbs in the first place, you'll reduce your number of unnecessary words. Change "She entered the room angrily" to "She stormed in." Auxiliary verbs (is, had,

were, etc.) often create a lot of sentence clutter. "They were wrestling." could be rewritten: "They wrestled."

17. **Read your stories out loud.** Read with feeling and use the different voices. Notice how the words flow, or don't flow. Are there any clumsy word combinations? ("She saw the sun shining on the salt shaker.") Dialog can be especially tricky. Read it carefully, out loud. Do all your characters sound alike? Would real people use the words you've given to your characters? Sometimes you can't answer these questions unless you hear your words read aloud.

18. **To write good dialog, use real language from real people.** If you're writing a story about a farmer, try to get next to a real farmer and listen to him talk. Notice the phrases he uses, the way he puts together his sentences. How does he use run-on sentences, fragments, contractions? You're doing a story about a bank manager? Listen to one. A bus driver? An auto mechanic? A nurse? Same thing. When you're writing dialog, it helps to know what's in each character's head, heart, and guts.

19. **If your story feels flat or lifeless, change the point of view.** If your story needs more juice, switch the narrator from first person to third person, or vice versa. If it's a children's story, turn that human family into a family of raccoons or ducks or zebras. If you don't like the result, change it back again. You are the one in control.

20. **Join a critique group.** As you work on your writing in class, your classmates are your critique group. They are your helpers, your lifeline. Outside of class, it's a good idea to have a few like-minded writer friends with whom you can share stories and feedback. That's what you call a critique group. Real writers belong to them. So should you.

Ten Things to Think About While You're Writing a Story

1. **Write with a particular reader in mind.** It could be your best friend, your mother, your cousin, someone you once knew and admired but haven't seen in a long time. Your writing will not please everyone, but it can — and will — tickle the fancy of a particular individual. And every individual thinks and feels much the same as hundreds of others with similar senses of humor, style, and wonder. So, if you can please *one person* with your writing, you will please hundreds, if not thousands, of others. (But you will *not* please everyone, so don't even try to do that.)

2. **Give the reader a good amount of information early in the story.** Novels used to begin with pages and pages of flowery description. Sometimes the main character, the person whose name was in the title of the book, wasn't introduced until Chapter 4. This is no longer acceptable. Today's readers want to know what's going on: Who is the main character? What kind of a person is he? What does he want? What is stopping him from getting it? Be careful, though, of overloading too much information at the very beginning. Let the readers know in Chapter 1 that the main character hopes with all his heart to win this year's fishing contest at Blue Lake. His motivations (he wants to make up for last year when he fell out of the boat, he wants to please his dying grandfather, he wants to impress the girl who moved in next door) can be explained later.

118

3. **Have more than one character desire something very badly.** Conflict is good. Characters with goals that clash make a story more complex and interesting.

4. **When writing fiction, save a few big secrets for the end.** In nonfiction, the main points are revealed immediately. News items cluster the names and results in the first paragraph or two, and give the details in the rest of the piece. With fiction, vital information — the solution to the mystery or an unexpected twist — is kept for the end. Readers want it that way.

5. **Create a main character who is likeable.** If your readers don't want the hero of your story to succeed, your story is doomed.

6. **Give your main character some questionable qualities.** And give the bad guy in your story some good points.

7. **Get your main character into a fix, and then make the difficult situation even worse before it gets better.** Your story needs to have ups and downs. When good things happen, the readers will begin to think the hero is in the clear. Then a crinkle occurs. How will the hero handle himself? The readers have a hunch that he is going to succeed, but they want to see (and approve of) how he pulls it off.

8. **Put the important words at the beginning or end of the sentence.** Change "From out of the woods the bear charged, and Justin jumped off the cliff, having no other choice." to "The bear charged out of the woods, and, having no other choice, Justin jumped off the cliff."

9. **Be careful of your tenses.** OK: "I <u>walked</u> into the room, and Mia <u>said</u> to me…" Also OK: "I <u>walk</u> into the room, and Mia <u>says</u> to me…" Not OK: "I <u>walked</u> into the room and Mia <u>says</u> to me…"

10. **Avoid using unnecessary words.** After you've written a first draft, go back and take out half of the words. Your story will most likely be much better. Compare these two sentences: "'It's me!' she said very

loudly and suddenly." "'It's me!' she blurted." The second sentence cuts the number of words in half and is clearer, cleaner, and easier to read. Note: Be careful also of overusing the exclamation mark. A writer should use exclamation marks the way a skilled driver uses the car's horn — not very often at all.

Grading Student Writing Assignments

Grading is not an integral part of the *We Think With Ink* program. Creative writing is *creative*; the finished products should not be given a rigid grade based on a checklist of do's and don'ts. Each writer has her own process and style; each story goes in its own direction.

With every assignment, your students are encouraged to venture into the wide-open spaces of their imaginations, and explore. Creativity and experimentation are sacrificed when we weigh our students down with the pressures of grading.

That said, if the powers-that-be at your school insist on a grade for creative work, follow these guidelines:

1. In checking a student's work — whether for a grade or not — be liberal with positive notes and messages of encouragement. Your students should look for your notes with eagerness. Highlight the well-written passages, examples of good word choice, and places where a technique learned in class has been used cleverly.

2. Hone the skill of scanning papers for positives, and force yourself to keep under control that eagle-eye for negatives. If there are twelve spelling mistakes, choose three or four that need immediate attention and write "sp" above them. If a single word is misspelled eight times in an assignment, don't mark each one. No writer wants to see a paper with red ink marking every single mistake. If your focus is primarily on what is wrong, your students will dread having their papers returned.

3. Grade just a fraction of the papers you assign; one of every four is usually sufficient. Allow students to submit papers of their choice. If a student wishes for more than one-fourth to be graded, honor the request.

120

*Learning how to write is a lot like learning
how to drive a car. With both, you must
pay attention to many things at once. The driver
must keep her eyes on the cars in front of
her as well as those behind, and those
converging from left and right. She must
keep her hands on the wheel, yet from time
to time must reach to work the gear
shift, or to turn on the windshield wiper,
or the lights. All the while, her feet are
working the pedals, and her eyes are
checking the mirrors and the speedometer
and the gas gauge and the stop lights up ahead...
At first it seems like too much for a person
to do all at once, but after a while much
of what needs to be done is accomplished
without much effort. The tasks of driving
become second nature. And that's how it
is with writing. With practice, you'll find
yourself breezing along without stopping
to consider where to place this comma,
how to finish that sentence, what letters
to use when spelling the difficult words
that once were so confusing...*

Ten Final Tips for Teachers

1. Call your students' parents with good news. Choose an evening and
   make five or six calls. Parents love hearing that someone thinks they
   have a great kid, that he's a pleasure to have in class, is fun, smart,
   respectful. A father I once called listened as I went on and on about his
   son. After a few minutes, the man impatiently cut me off and asked,
   "What is it you're calling about?" He thought I was buttering him up

with positives so the bad news that was coming wouldn't sting so much. When I told him there was no bad news, that I was calling just to tell him all those nice things, his whole attitude changed, he became more talkative, and ended the conversation by saying, "You're doing a hell of a job over there."

2. As much as possible, give kids choices. When giving an assignment, offer two or three ways to satisfy the requirements. Some people would prefer writing a paper about the signing of the Declaration of Independence, while others would jump at the chance to write a script and act out the scene for the class.

3. Give your students a chance to communicate with you in private by setting up a system that allows them to easily slip you a note. It doesn't take long to establish a system all will use and enjoy: "You give me a note, and I'll respond — usually with a compliment."

4. Don't be afraid to veer off on tangents while you're teaching, to drop what's being done, and elaborate on a comment or concern. Sometimes the most memorable moments in class occur when you're on a tangent.

5. Remind students often of their reason for being at school and of the many ways they are learning. As you return checked assignments, point out that just two short weeks ago, they didn't have the slightest idea how to accomplish the work at hand, but here now is evidence that they have learned. "You are learning a lot," is a good thing to hear. Students should hear those words frequently.

6. Point out often how the different subjects in school connect with each other. During science class, refer to math. During a language lesson, have the students recall what they're currently learning in social studies. By doing so, you are instilling a love of learning. No stray fact is wasted, and each little bit that is learned could be useful in a future writing project. To a writer, a fact is like a bandage in a first-aid kit — you never know when you will need it, and it just might save the day.

7. As your students are writing, ask questions that will help them to focus, but do this with care. If they are writing about people ice fishing, and you want your students to remember to describe the weather, don't ask, "Was it cold there on the lake?" A question that can be answered with a yes or a no will prompt your students to write lame sentences like, "It was cold." Instead, ask, "How cold was it on the lake?" or "How did the cold wind feel?"

8. Getting your students to write is not always easy. Sometimes it feels like you're moving boulders. Once a boulder starts to roll down a hill, however, it's hard to stop it, which brings us to another thing that isn't always easy: getting a writer to stop once she's got it going. The host of a TV talk show once famously admitted that on some nights "I just start talking until I have something to say." We writers sometimes have to just start writing until we have something to write. We write until something occurs to us, then we delete the early gibberish and go with the flow.

9. From time to time, throughout the school year, draw attention to the words from the first chapter of *We Think With Ink*. Remind the class of what we mean when we say those words: "We think with ink." Point to the messages and rules posted on the classroom walls and recall together why they are there and what they mean.

10. Allow your students to see how much you enjoy what you are doing each day, and how much you enjoy doing it with them. When you are reading and you come to a sentence or paragraph that blows you away, read it to the class so they can be blown away too. More important, get excited when you write an especially good sentence or paragraph. Share the excitement with your students, and call for them to do the same. We help each other to recognize when *magic is happening*.

"*Let us intoxicate ourselves with ink,*

since we lack the nectar of the gods."

— *Gustave Flaubert*

Appendix 1

Fillers

At the end of class, when you have just five or ten minutes and need a quick activity while waiting for the bell to ring, try one or two of these. Be sure to make time for the explanation of students' answers. If you have five minutes to fill, give the students just two minutes to record answers, leaving three minutes for sharing and discussion.

1. **Five-minute Lists:**
   a. "Write as many words as you can think of that start with 'w' and end with 'm.'" When time is up, ask for a volunteer to read her list. The words can be written on the board by a volunteer, or not. "Does anyone have a word that hasn't been said?" Take answers until there are no "new" words. (This activity can be varied endlessly by asking for words that start and end with different letters. To make it more difficult, specify that each word should contain a certain number of letters. "Make a list of five-letter words that start with 'b' and end with 'n.'")
   b. "Write a list of 5-letter words that don't start with 'sh' but have 'sh' in them somewhere."
   c. "Make a list of jobs/games/buildings that start with 'p' or 'l' or 'b' or..."
   d. "Make a list of contractions, or homonyms, or homophones, or synonyms for 'horrible' or 'tiny,' or antonyms for 'small' or 'loud'..."
   e. "Make a list of words that end with '-ough' or '-acing' or '-ire' or..."

2. **Root Word Fun:** Write a root word on the board ("read," "chair," "plant," etc.). Students are to make new words by adding prefixes, suffixes, and/or word parts ("reread," "reading," "reader," "mindreading," etc.). Who can come up with the most?

125

3. **Notice Anything?** "What do you notice about the following word(s)?" Give clues for what you want the students to notice.
   a. strength — has eight letters, yet only one vowel.
   b. facetious — has all five vowels, in alphabetical order.
   c. bookkeeper — a rare word with three sets of double letters in a row.
   d. write, sing, speak, come, eat, say, know, ride, see, grow — all have an irregular past tense: wrote, sang, spoke, came, ate, said, knew, rode, saw, grew (not writed, singed, speaked, comed, eated, sayed, knowed, rided, seed, growed).
   e. canopy, definition, first, hijack, sighing, stupendous — all contain three letters in alphabetical order ("canopy" has "n-o-p," "definition has "d-e-f," etc.).

4. **Letter Puzzle:** "What letter comes next in this sequence? B, C, D, E, G, P, T, V, ..." The answer is Z, the next letter said with a long "e" sound. (If doing this puzzle in England, Australia, or another of the countries where people say "zed," not "zee," end the series at "T" and expect an answer of "V.")

5. **Words with Many Meanings:** Choose a word with multiple meanings (round, down, fit, shake, fall, shot, pass, top, etc.). "Write a sentence with the word used as a noun. Now write a sentence with the word used as a verb. Can you write another sentence with the word used as an adjective or an adverb or some other way?" (The boxer was tired after the second round. The cowboy had to round up the cattle. I drew a circle that was perfectly round.) Variation: "Use the word as the first word in a sentence. Now use it as the last word in a sentence. Now use it as the middle word of a seven-word sentence."

6. **Which of These?**
   a. "Which of these is *not* a word? sew alot flounder finite" (alot)
   b. "Which of these is a homophone? thought through though cough." (through [threw])
   c. "Which of these is spelled correctly? curent rivver suggest Wendesday" (suggest)
   d. "Which of these is a plural? crisis index data oxen" (data, oxen)

126

7. **Make a List and Take It Apart:**
    a. "Make a list of five friends (or fruits or animals)."
    b. "How many different letters were used in your list?"
    c. "Which of your friends' names (or fruits or animals) has the most t's, a's, f's, etc.?"
    d. "Count the syllables of each. Which has the most?"

8. **Good Questions:** "Choose one of the following: cow, refrigerator, clock, TV, jar of jam. Now ask the object you've chosen as many questions as you can think of, starting each question with a different word." (Encourage the use of clauses. For example, "On the day you were first manufactured, what did you think was going to happen to you?"

Appendix 2

Daily Questions

The Daily Question, as described in Chapter 2, can be used as a class starter, something to get students thinking and writing while the teacher takes attendance, collects homework, or gets the class settled at the beginning of the hour. More than just a way to "get the rust off" the students' writing skills that may have lain dormant for many hours, the discussions generated by the Daily Question can be quite lively and provocative.

Here are some Daily Questions I have used. You can get additional mileage out of each one of the questions by changing a word or two. "How are you like a dog?" can be reused by changing "dog" to "cat" or another animal. For most questions, students are to write reasons for their answers ("a list of insects," obviously, won't require reasons). In time, add questions of your own to this list.

How are you like a dog?

Make a list of insects.

What makes someone a good person?

What are some different ways the adults you know show their feelings?

Make a list of plants that start with "r."

Are you more like a hawk, an owl, or a rooster?

Are you more like a car or a bicycle?

Which wild animal is like a member of your family?

What words do you like hearing at school?

Which invention was more important: the telephone or the car?

Make a list of mammals that start with "g," "l," or "t."

What is your favorite smell?

What was your favorite children's book when you were little?

What single word best describes your house?

How are you and your grandmother alike?

Appendix 3

Words of Wisdom (W.O.W.)

The Words of Wisdom, as described in Chapter 2, can be used in place of the Daily Question as a class starter. I used W.O.W. on Wednesdays only, and Daily Questions or curricula-based questions on the other days.

Listed below are 26 pieces of wisdom, chosen randomly from my files. You may, of course, use nuggets of wisdom you find on your own. And don't be surprised if your students start coming in with quotations they find in the books they are reading, or ones they themselves create.

The quotations below have been selected not only to trigger thought, but to introduce students to some of the great thinkers in history. Words of Wisdom quotations motivate without nagging or scolding. We use them to inspire, to boost self-esteem, to make thinkers *think*.

For each W.O.W., ask your students to explain, in a sentence or two, how the quotation makes them feel, if they agree with the statement, or what they suppose the writer had in mind when he wrote it. Students don't have to fully understand the quotation to write a sentence about it.

The last three on the list are related to writing, and may be used to provide a boost for writers needing a bit of motivation.

Nobody in here has to be perfect.

Start the school year with this one. Kids need to know that mistakes are allowed in the classroom, and that the teacher makes mistakes also. Let's just get it right out there in the open. With no one's name beneath this statement, students may assume that this is a direct message to them from the teacher in charge. Keep this quotation above your classroom door throughout the year.

Nothing is ugly that has life.
– Auguste Rodin

I always kept a tank in the back of the classroom with a resident toad or two, or a snake or a turtle or some other critter we cared for temporarily. I tried to instill in the students the sentiment expressed by the artist Rodin. An artist ought to know the meaning of beauty, right? So take a good look at that toad. Ugly, you say? No, it is not! If looked at closely and with an open mind — pretend you're another toad, if you must — much beauty is there to behold.

> **A real friend is one who walks in when the rest of the world walks out.**
> **— Walter Winchell**

Kids are always interested in the topic of friendship.

> **The great thing about getting older is that you don't lose**
> **all the other ages you've been.**
> **— Madeleine L'Engle**

It is good for young people to occasionally get a glimpse of the world from the perspective of the elderly.

> **All's well that ends well.**
> **— William Shakespeare**

This is a good one to use on a Friday. The week is over. Any hard feelings or troubles that arose earlier in the week are forgotten. Let's have a good day today so we can fully enjoy the weekend.

> **Make haste slowly.**
> **— Ben Franklin**

This one confuses students, but that's the beauty of some quotations. They make us *think*.

> **In the end it will be good. If it isn't good, it's not the end.**
> **— Anonymous**

Middle school students especially like the optimism of this one. I like to use it as a way of introducing the idea of "Anonymous," to whom many pieces of wisdom are attributed. Why would someone smart enough to think of something so wise or clever not put her name on it?

If you want to be a good student, you must do the things good students do.
— Michael Leannah

Sometimes the obvious needs to be said. If you want to be a good saxophone player, you must play the saxophone. If you want to be a good artist, you must get out the paints now and then. And if you want others to think of you as a good student, you must study, read, think, and do all the other things a good student does. And yes, this one was written by me, the teacher. It's good for the class to see that ordinary people can produce quotations worthy of analysis. After this one goes up each year, students usually start generating quotations of their own to be considered for Words of Wisdom.

Music should be something that makes you gotta move, inside or outside.
— Elvis Presley

I like this one because it shows that the English language can be mangled a bit and still produce a meaningful message. And it's always interesting to see what young people today know of Elvis Presley.

You cannot step into the same river twice.
— Heraclitus

A good message for anyone feeling bored. For some people, the days might seem repetitive, but with the right frame of mind, each day is obviously very different from the next.

Two things are infinite: the universe and human stupidity;
and I'm not sure about the universe.
— Albert Einstein

I believe Einstein said this after the creation of the atomic bomb. I use this at Halloween time and talk a bit about Frankenstein's monster.

We Think With Ink

I was not leaving the south to forget the south,
but so that someday I might understand it.
— Richard Wright

Richard Wright was a black man writing about leaving the south and all the problems and complexities it meant for him. But this quotation can strike a chord with anyone who is facing the fact that she must get away from what is familiar in order to fully grasp its meaning.

To use bitter words when kind words are at hand is like
picking unripe fruit when the ripe fruit is there.
— Thiruvalluvar

Thiruvalluvar was an ancient poet. His words, written so long ago, remind us that when we speak, it matters which words we choose to use.

The family is like a free university.
— Eknath Easwaran

Young people learn everything from gardening skills and cooking methods to sportsmanship and good humor from those at home, their parents and grandparents in particular.

Children need love, especially when they don't deserve it.
— Harold Hulbert

All kids like this one.

My mother had a great deal of trouble with me,
but I think she enjoyed it.
— Mark Twain

You can see why they like this one too.

We Think With Ink

Families are like fudge: mostly sweet with a few nuts.
— Anonymous

I always add that if you don't agree with this one, if no one comes to mind when you think about your family, then you must be one of the nuts.

The man is richest whose pleasures are the cheapest.
— Henry David Thoreau

Use this one at Christmas time.

I don't see problems as a problem.
— Mike Sherman

Mike Sherman was the head coach of the Green Bay Packers, and, though not as successful as Vince Lombardi, he displayed some real wisdom with these words, uttered after a game in which an injury occurred to an important player. We really ought to wake up each day expecting problems, so when they arise, we won't be thrown off course. We'll just take care of them and move on.

I will not take "but" for an answer.
— Langston Hughes

Most kids have heard the phrase, "I will not take 'no' for an answer." Hughes flips that common refrain on its side. With a little thinking, we can figure out what he was trying to say, especially if we know a bit about him and his poetry.

Few things are commonplace in themselves.
It's our reaction to them that grows dull.
— Arthur Gordon

Everyone needs this reminder once in a while. It's the small things in our world that make life truly wonderful. Sometimes they're so small and "insignificant" that we fail to notice them.

133

Each day as I look, I wonder where my eyes were yesterday.
— Bernard Berenson

Similar to the previous one. I use both of these, separated by several weeks.

In small matters trust the mind, in large ones the heart.
— Sigmund Freud

It's good for all kids to know a little something about Freud.

A writer is someone for whom writing is
more difficult than it is for other people.
— Thomas Mann

It's difficult for us because, while others just dash off sentences and let them stand, we writers wrestle with plot construction and agonize over the words we choose, sometimes to the point of being physically and mentally exhausted.

No surprise in the writer, no surprise in the reader.
— Robert Frost

If you have an open mind as you write, your characters might take you to unexpected places.

Nothing you write, if you hope to be any good,
will ever come out as you first hoped.
— Lillian Hellman

This is a cruel truth that is hard for the beginning writer to understand. Ideas and images in our brains do not often translate directly to the printed page. It takes much work, and many failed tries, to get across the feelings we attempt to express with our words.

Appendix 4

Fix-It Sentences

Fix-it Sentences can be used as a filler or as a separate, distinct activity. Write three flawed sentences on the board and ask the students to fix the mistakes. To increase the challenge, mix in a perfectly-written sentence from time to time.

Students will often suggest fixing something in a sentence that does not need to be fixed: "'The boy was talking to loud.' should be 'The boy was shouting to loud.'" To that you can say, "Good thinking, but 'talking' isn't incorrect. Look for something else in the sentence that needs fixing."

I sometimes got material for this activity from the students themselves. If I heard someone misusing the language, it became a Fix-it Sentence. Using Fix-it Sentences in this way heightens language awareness and corrects everyday grammar problems without drawing unnecessary attention to them.

The following list will get you started. Add examples of your own, as needed. Note: To reinforce correct usage, Fix-it Sentences can be reused by simply changing some of the names or words. For example, reuse #15 — "Where's Joey and Gina at?" — by reworking it into "Where is my pencil at?" or "Where's Carlos at tonight?"

1. I should of went with them. (I should have gone with them.)

2. Her and him are coming with us. (She and he are coming with us. Or: They are coming with us.)

3. I am going down to Green Bay next weekend. (I am going up to Green Bay next weekend.) Note: This one teaches geography more than good English. Discuss why someone from New York should not say, "I'm going up to Florida next week." For your purposes, choose a city that is north or south of you and write that you are going to go "up" or "down" to get there, leaving your students to use their geography skills to fix the sentence. (Traveling uphill or downhill is, of course, another matter.)

4. I could care less about your troubles. (I couldn't care less about your troubles.)

5. I bought ice cream chocolate cookies and vanilla wafers. (I bought ice cream, chocolate cookies, and vanilla wafers. Or: I bought ice, cream, chocolate, cookies, and vanilla wafers.)

6. I am going to get a hair cut today. (I am going to get a haircut today.) Note: If the writer of the sentence is going to get one single hair snipped, then the original sentence is fully correct.

7. We're gonna have a party at are house. (We're going to have a party at our house.)

8. I would of come over but it started to rain. (I would have come over, but it started to rain.)

9. "Can I go to the bathroom?" asked Mark. ("May I go to the bathroom?" asked Mark.) Note: Under unusual circumstances, the original sentence is correct.

10. Who's book is this on the table? (Whose book is this on the table?)

11. I should have went to their house when their cousins were there. (I should have gone to their house when their cousins were there.)

12. I have a yellow pencil, it needs to be sharpened. (I have a yellow pencil. It needs to be sharpened.)

13. I borrowed her my book so she could do the assignment. (I lent her my book so she could do the assignment. Note: "loaned" is also okay.)

14. Me and him played baseball yesterday night. (He and I played baseball last night.)

15. Where's Joey and Gina at?   (Where are Joey and Gina?)

16. Jolinda and Sam and Liz and Floyd are coming to my party tomorrow.
(Jolinda, Sam, Liz, and Floyd are coming to my party tomorrow.)

17. Where are we going to?   (Where are we going?)

18. Her and Meng ain't gonna be on time. (She and Meng aren't going to be
on time.)

19. Them gloves are to big for me. (Those gloves are too big for me.)

20. My brother don't care if I use his football. (My brother doesn't care if I
use his football.)

Appendix 5

Word Wall Lists

These word lists can be used for games in the classroom, for word walls or bulletin boards, or for lessons on word usage and word meaning.

Homophones

Homophones are words that sound alike, but have different meanings. Many games, puns, and riddles involve homophones. Leave room on the "Homophone Bulletin Board" for students to add more. (Point out the difficulty in alphabetizing the homophones. Should "hole/whole" go under "h" or "w"?)

air/heir	allowed/aloud	ate/eight
bored/board	break/brake	by/buy
course/coarse	deer/dear	fare/fair
find/fined	flee/flea	grate/great
groan/grown	guest/guessed	hair/hare
hall/haul	heel/heal	here/hear
hire/higher	hole/whole	idol/idle
I'll/aisle/isle	knight/night	loan/lone
made/maid	main/mane	mind/mined
minor/miner	need/knead/kneed	new/knew/gnu
no/know	nun/none	pail/pale
piece/peace	pier/peer	plain/plane
rap/wrap	ring/wring	rode/road
seen/scene	sent/cent/scent	so/sew
some/sum	steel/steal	son/sun
there/their/they're	threw/through	to/too/two
wade/weighed	waste/waist	way/weigh
week/weak	wood/would	you'll/Yule

Homographs

Homographs are words with different meanings that are spelled exactly
alike. A pair of homographs may or may not sound alike.

bass	bat	bank
bear	bow	change
compact	conduct	desert
die	down	evening
fire	grip	hand
just	lead	letter
light	live	match
mind	minute	nail
number	park	polish
present	project	read
refuse	resume	rock
rose	row	second
sewer	sink	spoke
story	subject	tear
type	watch	wave
wind	wound	yarn

We Think With Ink

Vocabulary Words

You might wish to use a bulletin board or word wall to display a list of words from a book or chapter being used in class. For example, the list below was compiled from a book my students were assigned to read. Referring to the list on the wall helped to increase fluency and comprehension. With the start of a new book or chapter, clear the wall for a new set of words.

daring	lenient	timid
optimistic	pessimistic	assured
clutch	debatable	easygoing
erroneous	expectant	promote
hearten	insurgent	liberal
permissive	rebellious	unresolved

Idioms

"Mr. Jones kicked the bucket" is another way of saying that Mr. Jones has *died*. "Kick the bucket" is one of the many idioms that are part of the English language. Idioms can be tricky, because they say one thing and mean something else. They are like a secret code, making sense only if we know their hidden meanings.

Idioms add color and spice to what we say and write, but we must be careful with them. What would a person unfamiliar with the idiom — someone just learning our language, for instance — think when hearing that someone "kicked the bucket"?

One way to make use of idioms in the classroom is to choose one and do research to learn how the saying got started. Finding the origins of idioms can be a lot of fun. Why, for instance, do people go "nuts" or "bananas," but never "raisins" or "papayas"?

Make a word wall or fill a bulletin board with the idioms below. As with other such lists, ask students to be on the look-out for more.

She brought home the bacon.	Don't spill the beans.
Don't upset the apple cart.	Take it with a grain of salt.
She's rolling in the dough.	That hit the spot.

We Think With Ink

Don't burn the candle at both ends.   He has ants in his pants.
She was laughing her head off.   Let's shoot the breeze.
Don't put all your eggs in one basket.   We chewed the fat.
You won't have to twist my arm.   He really got my goat.
They let the cat out of the bag.   He had us in stitches.
I beat him to the punch.   He is off his rocker.
I'll take a crack at it.   He's feeling blue.
She's down in the dumps.   He had egg on his face.
I think I'll catch some z's.   I'm off the hook.
Are you pulling my leg?   It's a piece of cake.
She's in over her head.   He's green with envy.
He's chomping at the bit.   Don't jump the gun.
I got up on the wrong side of the bed.   It made my blood boil.
He threw a monkey wrench into the works. He got cold feet.

Clichés

We usually use word walls and bulletin boards to display examples of good language and vocabulary, but sometimes we can use them to show what writers ought to avoid. Clichés, for instance.

Clichés are phrases that have been overused and have lost their zing. They make our writing predictable and boring, allowing readers to finish sentences without reading them to the end. "He was as slow as a turtle." There is nothing grammatically wrong with that sentence, and at one time that phrase was fresh and good, but it has grown old and stale. It doesn't necessarily have to be entirely scrapped, however. If it can be changed into something the reader won't anticipate, then we're good to go: "He was as slow as a turtle tromping through wet cement."

What a pain in the neck.   …as far as the eye can see.
He's afraid of his own shadow.   He's as happy as a clam.
She was as white as a sheet.   He cried like a baby.
I'm as free as a bird.   …quick as a flash.
Let's not reinvent the wheel.   He's as strong as an ox.
I stood out like a sore thumb.   That was easy as pie.
He's as nutty as a fruitcake.   It lasted an eternity.

141

Weird Words

The words below have weird spelling patterns, funny pronunciations, or something else that makes them irregular. In short, they break the rules of the English language. In fact, if we arrested all the words that break the rules of good English the way we arrest people who break the rules of society, the jails would be full. For instance, why doesn't "Wednesday" sound the way it is spelled? Why in the world does "bread" have a short "e" sound? Why doesn't "one" rhyme with "bone"? Why doesn't "stove" rhyme with either "move" or "love"? What about "tomb," "bomb," and "comb"?

Weird words are fun to spot in books and magazines. This bulletin board or word wall ought to fill up quickly with student contributions.

some	colonel	aisle
breakfast	shoe	iron
island	answer	rhythm
choir	gnat	doubt
hour	climb	blood

cough/though/through/rough/bough

Suggested Reading

If I were to recommend five good books on writing, grammar, and word play, I would be guilty of negligence for failing to cite so many others. We are lucky to have such a vast array of reliable old standbys, with new gems published every year. Seek and ye shall find a collection of books waiting for a permanent home on your shelf.

From where I sit as I write this today, I see a copy of Patricia T. O'Conner's *Woe is I*, a book I turn to when wrestling over the difference between "continuous" and "continual," or other such language befuddlements. Everyone needs a survival guide like that one.

I also see books by John Gardner, Anne Lamott, Noah Lukeman, Richard Lederer, William Safire, Sol Stein, Bill Bryson, and many more.

Of course, Strunk and White's *The Elements of Style* has a prominent place. I recommend it for a place at your desk, too.

About the Author

Michael Leannah has more than thirty years' experience as a teacher in elementary and middle schools. He writes fiction and nonfiction for children and adults. He is the award-winning author of *Something for Everyone: Memories of Lauerman Brothers Department Store*, a local history. Leannah is also the author of the children's picture books *Most People, Goodnight Whispers,* and *Farmer Huckinshuck's Wild Ride.* His children's stories have appeared in magazines in the United States and Australia. His award-winning radio plays have been performed in many cities. He lives in Sheboygan, Wisconsin.

Please visit:
wethinkwithink.com
michaelleannah.com

Index

Game Index

Name Index

And now, on to the next thing…